John Milton

Paradise Lost
Books I and II

✳

Edited by Anna Baldwin

Oxford University Press

for my father, John Barber

Oxford University Press, Great Clarendon Street, Oxford OX2 6DP

Oxford New York
Athens Auckland Bangkok Bogota Buenos Aires
Calcutta Cape Town Chennai Dar es Salaam Delhi
Florence Hong Kong Istanbul Karachi Kuala Lumpur
Madrid Melbourne Mexico City Mumbai Nairobi
Paris São Paulo Singapore Taipei Tokyo Toronto Warsaw

and associated companies in
Berlin Ibadan

Oxford is a trade mark of Oxford University Press

© Notes, and Approaches:
Anna Baldwin 1998

First published by Oxford University Press
ISBN 0 19 832001 9

Other titles in the series

Blake: Songs of Innocence and of Experience	0 19 831952 5
Chaucer: General Prologue to the Canterbury Tales	0 19 831967 3
Chaucer: The Miller's Tale	0 19 831988 6
Chaucer: The Nun's Priest's Tale	0 19 831987 8
John Donne: Selected Poems	0 19 831950 9
Robert Frost: Selected Poems	0 19 832002 7
Christopher Fry: The Lady's Not For Burning	0 19 831959 2
Thomas Hardy: Selected Poems	0 19 831963 0
Gerard Manley Hopkins: Selected Poems	0 19 831961 4
D.H. Lawrence: Selected Poems	0 19 831962 2
Alexander Pope: The Rape of the Lock	0 19 831958 4
Six Women Poets	0 19 833181 9
William Wordsworth: Selected Poems	0 19 881951 7
W.B. Yeats: Selected Poems	0 19 831966 5
19th & 20th Century Women Poets	0 19 831990 8

Typeset by AFS Image Setters Ltd, Glasgow

Printed and bound in Great Britain

The publishers would like to thank the following for permission to
reproduce photographs:

p. 191 (top) Archivi Alinari; p. 192 British Library (Ms Cotton Nero CIV fol 39r);
p. 193 The Prado, Madrid/Bridgeman Art Library, London; p. 194 (bottom)
© The British Museum

Artwork on p. 191 (bottom) by Oxford Illustrators

The cover illustration is by John Ashton.

Contents

Contents

Contents

Acknowledgements

Although the text has been re-edited for this edition, this task, like that of compiling the Notes, has been enormously assisted by the work of previous scholars. I would like to pay particular tribute to the editions of *Paradise Lost I and II* by F.T. Prince (Oxford University Press, 1962), which this edition will replace, and by John Broadbent (Cambridge University Press, 1972). They are both inspirational as well as informative, and I have often plundered their wisdom. I have quoted other parts of Paradise Lost from the edition by Alastair Fowler, in *The Works of John Milton*, edited by John Carey and Alastair Fowler (Longman, 1968), which is also full of useful insights, and I have more occasionally used that by Merritt Hughes (*Odyssey*, 1977) and older ones by Rajan, Verity, and others. I have quoted the prose works from *John Milton: Selected Prose* edited by C.A. Patrides (Penguin, 1974). Most of the secondary sources I have used are cited in the section on *Further Reading*. I would also like to thank Victor Lee and all those who read and commented on the book, notably Ellen Lambert, John and Stephen Barber.

We are grateful for permission to reprint the following copyright texts in the appendix:

Extracts from the *Authorized Version of the Bible (The King James Bible)*, the rights in which are vested in the Crown, are reproduced by permission of the Crown's Patentee, Cambridge University Press.

Slightly adapted extract from Jean Paul Sartre: *In Camera (Huis Clos)* translated by Stuart Gilbert (Hamish Hamilton, 1946), translation copyright © 1946 by Stuart Gilbert, is reprinted by permission of Penguin Books Ltd.

Anna Baldwin

Editors

Dr Victor Lee, the series editor, read English at University College, Cardiff. He was later awarded his doctorate at the University of Oxford. He has taught at secondary and tertiary level, and worked for twenty-seven years at the Open University. Victor Lee's experience as an examiner is very wide: he has been a Chief Examiner in English A-level for three different boards stretching over a period of almost thirty years.

Dr Anna Baldwin gained an MA and a PhD in English from Girton College, Cambridge, and went on to lecture in the Department of English and Related Literature at the University of York for 14 years. In 1994, following a family move back to Cambridge, she took her PGCE at Cambridge University and has been teaching A-level English Literature at Hills Rd. Sixth Form College, Cambridge, ever since. Her other books are *The Theme of Government in Piers Plowman* (1981) and *Platonism and the English Imagination* (co-edited with Sarah Hutton, 1994) which includes an article by her on Milton.

Foreword

Oxford Student Texts are specifically aimed at presenting poetry and drama to an audience which is studying English Literature at an advanced level. Each text is designed as an integrated whole consisting of three main parts. The poetry or the play is placed first to stress its importance and to encourage students to enjoy it without secondary critical material of any kind. When help is needed on other occasions, the second and third parts of these texts, the Notes and the Approaches, provide it.

The Notes perform two functions. First, they provide information and explain allusions. Secondly, and this is where they differ from most texts at this level, they often raise questions of central concern to the interpretation of the poem or the play being dealt with, particularly in the use of a general note placed at the beginning of the particular notes.

The third part, the Approaches section, deals with major issues of response to the particular selection of poetry or drama, as opposed to the work of the writer as a whole. One of the major aims of this part of the text is to emphasize that there is no one right answer or interpretation, but a series of approaches. Readers are given guidance as to what counts as evidence, but, in the end, left to make up their mind as to which are the most suitable interpretations, or to add their own.

To help achieve this, the Approaches section contains a number of activity-discussion sequences, although it must be stressed that these are optional. Significant issues about the poem or the play are raised in these activities. Readers are invited to tackle these activities before proceeding to the discussion section where possible responses to the questions raised in the activities are considered. Their main function is to engage readers actively in the ideas of the text. However, these activity-discussion sequences are so arranged that, if readers wish to treat the Approaches as continuous prose and not attempt the activities, they can.

At the end of each text there is also a list of Tasks. Whereas the activity-discussion sequences are aimed at increasing understanding of the literary work itself, these tasks are intended to help explore ideas about the poetry or the play after the student has completed the reading of the work and the studying of the Notes and Approaches. These tasks are particularly helpful for coursework projects or in preparing for an examination.

Victor Lee   *Series Editor*

A Note on the Text

The text is based on the first edition (1667) though I have removed all capitals except those which denote proper names (for example, *Heaven* when it means God's home rather than the sky) and God himself (for example, *the Thunderer*), all italics, and all archaic spellings and contractions of words except those which affect the metre (for example, *th'Eternal*). I have followed John Broadbent (Cambridge University Press, 1972), though much more sparingly, in adding the occasional accent where a modern pronunciation would affect metre. Punctuation has been retained (except for the addition of one or two question marks and full stops), but as Milton used commas, semi-colons, colons, and full stops in ascending order to denote the greater length of the pauses the voice should make when reading the poem aloud, do not expect them to help very much with conveying the grammar.

The Notes which start on p.56 are divided into sections, and I have made breaks in the text to indicate where each section begins.

Book I

Of Man's first disobedience, and the fruit
Of that forbidden tree, whose mortal taste
Brought death into the world, and all our woe,
With loss of Eden, till one greater Man
5   Restore us, and regain the blissful seat,
Sing heavenly Muse, that on the secret top
Of Oreb, or of Sinai, didst inspire
That shepherd who first taught the chosen seed,
In the beginning how the heavens and earth
10   Rose out of Chaos; or if Sion hill
Delight thee more, and Siloa's brook that flowed
Fast by the oracle of God: I thence
Invoke thy aid to my adventurous song,
That with no middle flight intends to soar
15   Above th'Aonian mount, while it pursues
Things unattempted yet in prose or rhyme.
And chiefly thou O Spirit, that dost prefer
Before all temples th'upright heart and pure,
Instruct me, for thou know'st; thou from the first
20   Wast present, and with mighty wings outspread
Dove-like sat'st brooding on the vast abyss
And mad'st it pregnant: what in me is dark
Illumine, what is low raise and support;
That to the highth of this great argument
25   I may assert eternal Providence,
And justify the ways of God to men.

Say first, for Heaven hides nothing from thy view
Nor the deep tract of Hell, say first what cause
Moved our grandparents in that happy state,
30   Favoured of heaven so highly, to fall off

From their Creator, and transgress his will
For one restraint, lords of the world besides?
Who first seduced them to that foul revolt?
Th'infernal serpent; he it was, whose guile
35   Stirred up with envy and revenge, deceived
The mother of Mankind, what time his pride
Had cast him out from Heaven, with all his host
Of rebel angels, by whose aid aspiring
To set himself in glory above his peers,
40   He trusted to have equalled the most High,
If he opposed; and with ambitious aim
Against the throne and monarchy of God
Raised impious war in heaven and battle proud
With vain attempt. Him the Almighty Power
45   Hurled headlong flaming from th'ethereal sky
With hideous ruin and combustion down
To bottomless perdition, there to dwell
In adamantine chains and penal fire,
Who durst defy the Omnipotent to arms.

50   Nine times the space that measures day and night
To mortal men, he with his horrid crew
Lay vanquished, rolling in the fiery gulf
Confounded though immortal. But his doom
Reserved him to more wrath; for now the thought
55   Both of lost happiness and lasting pain
Torments him; round he throws his baleful eyes
That witnessed huge affliction and dismay
Mixed with obdurate pride and steadfast hate:
At once as far as angels' ken he views
60   The dismal situation waste and wild,
A dungeon horrible, on all sides round
As one great furnace flamed, yet from those flames
No light, but rather darkness visible
Served only to discover sights of woe,

65   Regions of sorrow, doleful shades, where peace
        And rest can never dwell, hope never comes
        That comes to all; but torture without end
        Still urges, and a fiery deluge, fed
        With ever-burning sulphur unconsumed:
70   Such place eternal Justice had prepared
        For those rebellious, here their prison ordained
        In utter darkness, and their portion set
        As far removed from God and light of heaven
        As from the centre thrice to th'utmost pole.
75   O how unlike the place from whence they fell!
        There the companions of his fall, o'erwhelmed
        With floods and whirlwinds of tempestuous fire,
        He soon discerns, and weltering by his side
        One next himself in power, and next in crime,
80   Long after known in Palestine, and named
        Beëlzebub. To whom the arch-enemy,
        And thence in heaven called Satan, with bold words
        Breaking the horrid silence thus began.

Satan: 'If thou beest he; but O how fallen! how changed
85   From him, who in the happy realms of light
        Clothed with transcendent brightness didst outshine
        Myriads though bright: if he whom mutual league,
        United thoughts and counsels, equal hope,
        And hazard in the glorious enterprise,
90   Joined with me once, now misery hath joined
        In equal ruin: into what pit thou seest
        From what highth fallen, so much the stronger proved
        He with his thunder: and till then who knew
        The force of those dire arms? Yet not for those
95   Nor what the potent Victor in his rage
        Can else inflict, do I repent or change,
        Though changed in outward lustre, that fixed mind
        And high disdain, from sense of injured merit,

That with the mightiest raised me to contend,
100 And to the fierce contention brought along
Innumerable force of spirits armed
That durst dislike his reign, and me preferring,
His utmost power with adverse power opposed
In dubious battle on the plains of heaven,
105 And shook his throne. What though the field be lost?
All is not lost; th'unconquerable will,
And study of revenge, immortal hate,
And courage never to submit or yield:
And what is else not to be overcome?
110 That glory never shall his wrath or might
Extort from me. To bow and sue for grace
With suppliant knee, and deify his power
Who from the terror of this arm so late
Doubted his empire, that were low indeed,
115 That were an ignominy and shame beneath
This downfall; since by fate the strength of gods
And this empyreal substance cannot fail,
Since through experience of this great event
In arms not worse, in foresight much advanced,
120 We may with more successful hope resolve
To wage by force or guile eternal war
Irreconcilable to our grand Foe,
Who now triumphs, and in th'excess of joy
Sole reigning holds the tyranny of Heaven.'
125 So spake the apostate angel, though in pain,
Vaunting aloud, but racked with deep despair:

And him thus answered soon his bold compeer.
Beëlzebub: 'O prince, O chief of many thronèd powers
That led th'embattled seraphim to war
130 Under thy conduct, and in dreadful deeds
Fearless, endangered heaven's perpetual King;
And put to proof his high supremacy,

Whether upheld by strength, or chance, or fate;
Too well I see and rue the dire event,
135   That with sad overthrow and foul defeat
Hath lost us heaven, and all this mighty host
In horrible destruction laid thus low,
As far as gods and heavenly essences
Can perish: for the mind and spirit remains
140   Invincible, and vigour soon returns,
Though all our glory extinct, and happy state
Here swallowed up in endless misery.
But what if he our Conqueror, (whom I now
Of force believe Almighty, since no less
145   Than such could have o'erpowered such force as ours)
Have left us this our spirit and strength entire
Strongly to suffer and support our pains,
That we may so suffice his vengeful ire,
Or do him mightier service as his thralls
150   By right of war, whate'er his business be
Here in the heart of Hell to work in fire,
Or do his errands in the gloomy deep;
What can it then avail though yet we feel
Strength undiminished, or eternal being
155   To undergo eternal punishment?'

Whereto with speedy words the arch-fiend replied.
Satan: 'Fallen cherub, to be weak is miserable
Doing or suffering: but of this be sure,
To do aught good never will be our task,
160   But ever to do ill our sole delight,
As being the contrary to his high will
Whom we resist. If then his Providence
Out of our evil seek to bring forth good,
Our labour must be to pervert that end,
165   And out of good still to find means of evil;
Which oft-times may succeed, so as perhaps

Shall grieve him, if I fail not, and disturb
His inmost counsels from their destined aim.
But see the angry Victor hath recalled
170   His ministers of vengeance and pursuit
Back to the gates of heaven: the sulphurous hail
Shot after us in storm, o'erblown hath laid
The fiery surge, that from the precipice
Of heaven received us falling, and the thunder,
175   Winged with red lightning and impetuous rage,
Perhaps hath spent his shafts, and ceases now
To bellow through the vast and boundless deep.
Let us not slip th'occasion, whether scorn,
Or satiate fury yield it from our Foe.
180   Seest thou yon dreary plain, forlorn and wild,
The seat of desolation, void of light,
Save what the glimmering of these livid flames
Casts pale and dreadful? Thither let us tend
From off the tossing of these fiery waves,
185   There rest, if any rest can harbour there,
And reassembling our afflicted powers,
Consult how we may henceforth most offend
Our Enemy, our own loss how repair,
How overcome this dire calamity,
190   What reinforcement we may gain from hope,
If not what resolution from despair.'

Thus Satan talking to his nearest mate
With head up-lift above the wave, and eyes
That sparkling blazed, his other parts besides
195   Prone on the flood, extended long and large
Lay floating many a rood, in bulk as huge
As whom the fables name of monstrous size,
Titanian, or Earth-born, that warred on Jove,
Briareos or Typhon, whom the den
200   By ancient Tarsus held, or that sea-beast

Leviathan, which God of all his works
Created hugest that swim th'ocean stream:
Him haply slumbering on the Norway foam
The pilot of some small night-foundered skiff,
205 Deeming some island, oft, as seamen tell,
With fixèd anchor in his scaly rind
Moors by his side under the lea, while night
Invests the sea, and wishèd morn delays:
So stretched out huge in length the arch-fiend lay
210 Chained on the burning lake, nor ever thence
Had risen or heaved his head, but that the will
And high permission of all-ruling Heaven
Left him at large to his own dark designs,
That with reiterated crimes he might
215 Heap on himself damnation, while he sought
Evil to others, and enraged might see
How all his malice served but to bring forth
Infinite goodness, grace and mercy shown
On Man by him seduced, but on himself
220 Treble confusion, wrath and vengeance poured.
Forthwith upright he rears from off the pool
His mighty stature; on each hand the flames
Driven backward slope their pointing spires, and
    rolled
In billows leave i' th'midst a horrid vale.
225 Then with expanded wings he steers his flight
Aloft, incumbent on the dusky air
That felt unusual weight, till on dry land
He lights, if it were land that ever burned
With solid, as the lake with liquid fire;
230 And such appeared in hue, as when the force
Of subterranean wind transports a hill
Torn from Pelorus, or the shattered side
Of thundering Etna, whose combustible
And fuelled entrails thence conceiving fire,

235   Sublimed with mineral fury, aid the winds,
   And leave a singèd bottom all involved
   With stench and smoke: such resting found the sole
   Of unblessed feet. Him followed his next mate,
   Both glorying to have scaped the Stygian flood
240   As gods, and by their own recovered strength,
   Not by the sufferance of supernal Power.

Satan: 'Is this the region, this the soil, the clime,'
   Said then the lost archangel, 'this the seat
   That we must change for Heaven, this mournful gloom
245   For that celestial light? Be it so, since he
   Who now is sovereign can dispose and bid
   What shall be right: farthest from him is best
   Whom reason hath equalled, force hath made
    supreme
   Above his equals. Farewell happy fields
250   Where joy for ever dwells: hail horrors, hail
   Infernal world, and thou profoundest Hell
   Receive thy new possessor: one who brings
   A mind not to be changed by place or time.
   The mind is its own place, and in itself
255   Can make a Heaven of Hell, a Hell of Heaven.
   What matter where, if I be still the same,
   And what I should be, all but less than he
   Whom thunder hath made greater? Here at least
   We shall be free; th'Almighty hath not built
260   Here for his envy, will not drive us hence:
   Here we may reign secure, and in my choice
   To reign is worth ambition though in Hell:
   Better to reign in Hell, than serve in Heaven.
   But wherefore let we then our faithful friends
265   Th'associates and co-partners of our loss
   Lie thus astonished on th'oblivious pool,
   And call them not to share with us their part

In this unhappy mansion, or once more
With rallied arms to try what may be yet
270   Regained in Heaven, or what more lost in Hell?'
    So Satan spake, and him Beëlzebub
Thus answered.
Beëlzebub: 'Leader of those armies bright,
Which but th'Omnipotent none could have foiled,
If once they hear that voice, their liveliest pledge
275   Of hope in fears and dangers, heard so oft
In worst extremes, and on the perilous edge
Of battle when it raged, in all assaults
Their surest signal, they will soon resume
New courage and revive, though now they lie
280   Grovelling and prostrate on yon lake of fire,
As we erewhile, astounded and amazed,
No wonder, fallen such a pernicious highth.'

He scarce had ceased when the superior fiend
Was moving toward the shore; his ponderous shield
285   Ethereal temper, massy, large and round,
Behind him cast; the broad circumference
Hung on his shoulders like the moon, whose orb
Through optic glass the Tuscan artist views
At evening from the top of Fésolè,
290   Or in Valdarno, to descry new lands,
Rivers or mountains in her spotty globe.
His spear, to equal which the tallest pine
Hewn on Norwegian hills, to be the mast
On some great ammiral, were but a wand
295   He walked with to support uneasy steps
Over the burning marl, not like those steps
On heaven's azure, and the torrid clime
Smote on him sore besides, vaulted with fire;
Nathless he so endured, till on the beach
300   Of that inflamèd sea, he stood and called

His legions, angel forms, who lay entranced
Thick as autumnal leaves that strow the brooks
In Vallombrosa, where th'Etrurian shades
High overarched embower; or scattered sedge
305 Afloat, when with fierce winds Orion armed
Hath vexed the Red Sea coast, whose waves o'erthrew
Busiris and his Memphian chivalry,
While with perfidious hatred they pursued
The sojourners of Goshen, who beheld
310 From the safe shore their floating carcasses
And broken chariot wheels, so thick bestrown
Abject and lost lay these, covering the flood,
Under amazement of their hideous change.
He called so loud, that all the hollow deep
315 Of Hell resounded.

Satan: 'Princes, potentates,
Warriors, the flower of Heaven, once yours, now lost,
If such astonishment as this can seize
Eternal spirits; or have ye chosen this place
After the toil of battle to repose
320 Your wearied virtue, for the ease you find
To slumber here, as in the vales of Heaven?
Or in this abject posture have ye sworn
T'adore the Conqueror? who now beholds
Cherub and seraph rolling in the flood
325 With scattered arms and ensigns, till anon
His swift pursuers from Heaven gates discern
Th'advantage, and descending tread us down
Thus drooping, or with linkèd thunderbolts
Transfix us to the bottom of this gulf.
330 Awake, arise, or be for ever fallen.'

They heard, and were abashed, and up they sprung
Upon the wing, as when men wont to watch
On duty, sleeping found by whom they dread,

Rouse and bestir themselves ere well awake.
335 Nor did they not perceive the evil plight
In which they were, or the fierce pains not feel;
Yet to their general's voice they soon obeyed
Innumerable. As when the potent rod
Of Amram's son in Egypt's evil day
340 Waved round the coast, up called a pitchy cloud
Of locusts, warping on the eastern wind,
That o'er the realm of impious Pharaoh hung
Like night, and darkened all the land of Nile:
So numberless were those bad angels seen
345 Hovering on wing under the cope of Hell
'Twixt upper, nether, and surrounding fires;
Till, as a signal given, th'uplifted spear
Of their great sultan waving to direct
Their course, in even balance down they light
350 On the firm brimstone, and fill all the plain;
A multitude, like which the populous North
Poured never from her frozen loins, to pass
Rhene or the Danaw, when her barbarous sons
Came like a deluge on the South, and spread
355 Beneath Gibraltar to the Libyan sands.
Forthwith from every squadron and each band
The heads and leaders thither haste where stood
Their great commander; godlike shapes and forms
Excelling human, princely dignities,
360 And powers that erst in heaven sat on thrones;
Though of their names in heavenly records now
Be no memorial, blotted out and rased
By their rebellion, from the Books of Life.
Nor had they yet among the sons of Eve
365 Got them new names, till wandering o'er the Earth,
Through God's high sufferance for the trial of Man,
By falsities and lies the greatest part
Of Mankind they corrupted to forsake

God their creator, and th'invisible
370 Glory of him, that made them, to transform
Oft to the image of a brute, adorned
With gay religions full of pomp and gold,
And devils to adore for deities:
Then were they known to men by various names,
375 And various idols through the heathen world.

Say, Muse, their names then known, who first, who
    last,
Roused from the slumber on that fiery couch,
At their great emperor's call, as next in worth
Came singly where he stood on the bare strand,
380 While the promiscuous crowd stood yet aloof?
The chief were those who from the pit of Hell
Roaming to seek their prey on Earth, durst fix
Their seats long after next the seat of God,
Their altars by his altar, gods adored
385 Among the nations round, and durst abide
Jehovah thundering out of Sion, throned
Between the cherubim; yea, often placed
Within his sanctuary itself their shrines,
Abominations; and with cursèd things
390 His holy rites, and solemn feasts profaned,
And with their darkness durst affront his light.
First Moloch, horrid king besmeared with blood
Of human sacrifice, and parents' tears,
Though for the noise of drums and timbrels loud
395 Their children's cries unheard, that passed through
    fire
To his grim idol. Him the Ammonite
Worshipped in Rabba and her watery plain,
In Argob and in Basan, to the stream
Of utmost Arnon. Nor content with such
400 Audacious neighbourhood, the wisest heart

Of Solomon he led by fraud to build
His temple right against the temple of God
On that opprobrious hill, and made his grove
The pleasant valley of Hinnom, Tophet thence
405 And black Gehenna called, the type of Hell.
Next Chemos, th'obscene dread of Moab's sons,
From Aroar to Nebo, and the wild
of southmost Abarim; in Hesebon
And Horonaïm, Seon's realm, beyond
410 The flowery dale of Sibma clad with vines,
And Elealè to th'asphaltic pool.
Peor his other name, when he enticed
Israel in Sittim on their march from Nile,
To do him wanton rites, which cost them woe.
415 Yet thence his lustful orgies he enlarged
Even to that hill of scandal, by the grove
Of Moloch homicide, lust hard by hate;
Till good Josiah drove them thence to Hell.
With these came they, who from the bordering flood
420 Of old Euphrates to the brook that parts
Egypt from Syrian ground, had general names
Of Baälim and Ashtaroth, those male,
These feminine. For spirits when they please
Can either sex assume, or both; so soft
425 And uncompounded is their essence pure,
Not tied or manacled with joint or limb,
Nor founded on the brittle strength of bones,
Like cumbrous flesh; but in what shape they choose
Dilated or condensed, bright or obscure,
430 Can execute their airy purposes,
And works of love or enmity fulfil.
For those the race of Israel oft forsook
Their living strength, and unfrequentèd left
His righteous altar, bowing lowly down
435 To bestial gods; for which their heads as low

Bowed down in battle, sunk before the spear
Of despicable foes. With these in troop
Came Astoreth, whom the Phoenicians called
Astartè, queen of heaven, with crescent horns;
440   To whose bright image nightly by the moon
Sidonian virgins paid their vows and songs,
In Sion also not unsung, where stood
Her temple on th'offensive mountain, built
By that uxorious king, whose heart though large,
445   Beguiled by fair idolatresses, fell
To idols foul. Thammuz came next behind,
Whose annual wound in Lebanon allured
The Syrian damsels to lament his fate
In amorous ditties all a summer's day,
450   While smooth Adonis from his native rock
Ran purple to the sea, supposed with blood
Of Thammuz yearly wounded: the love-tale
Infected Sion's daughters with like heat,
Whose wanton passions in the sacred porch
455   Ezekiel saw, when by the vision led
His eye surveyed the dark idolatries
Of alienated Judah. Next came one
Who mourned in earnest, when the captive Ark
Maimed his brute image, head and hands lopped off
460   In his own temple, on the grunsel edge,
Where he fell flat, and shamed his worshippers:
Dagon his name, sea monster, upward man
And downward fish: yet had his temple high
Reared in Azotus, dreaded through the coast
465   Of Palestine, in Gath and Ascalon,
And Accaron and Gaza's frontier bounds.
Him followed Rimmon, whose delightful seat
Was fair Damascus, on the fertile banks
Of Abbana and Pharphar, lucid streams.
470   He also against the house of God was bold:

A leper once he lost and gained a king,
Ahaz his sottish conqueror, whom he drew
God's altar to disparage and displace
For one of Syrian mode, whereon to burn
475   His odious offerings, and adore the gods
Whom he had vanquished. After these appeared
A crew who under names of old renown,
Osiris, Isis, Orus and their train
With monstrous shapes and sorceries abused
480   Fanatic Egypt and her priests, to seek
Their wandering gods disguised in brutish forms
Rather than human. Nor did Israel scape
Th'infection when their borrowed gold composed
The calf in Oreb: and the rebel king
485   Doubled that sin in Bethel and in Dan,
Likening his Maker to the grazèd ox,
Jehovah, who in one night when he passed
From Egypt marching, equalled with one stroke
Both her first born and all her bleating gods.
490   Belial came last, than whom a spirit more lewd
Fell not from heaven, or more gross to love
Vice for itself: to him no temple stood
Or altar smoked; yet who more oft than he
In temples and at altars, when the priest
495   Turns atheist, as did Eli's sons, who filled
With lust and violence the house of God?
In courts and palaces he also reigns
And in luxurious cities, where the noise
Of riot ascends above their loftiest towers,
500   And injury and outrage: and when night
Darkens the streets, then wander forth the sons
Of Belial, flown with insolence and wine.
Witness the streets of Sodom, and that night
In Gibeah, when the hospitable door
505   Exposed a matron to avoid worse rape.

These were the prime in order and in might;
The rest were long to tell, though far renowned,
The Ionian gods, of Javan's issue held
Gods, yet confessed later than Heaven and Earth
510 Their boasted parents; Titan Heaven's first born
With his enormous brood, and birthright seized
By younger Saturn, he from mightier Jove
His own and Rhea's son like measure found;
So Jove usurping reigned: these first in Crete
515 And Ida known, thence on the snowy top
Of cold Olympus ruled the middle air
Their highest heaven; or on the Delphian cliff,
Or in Dodona, and through all the bounds
Of Doric land; or who with Saturn old
520 Fled over Adria to th'Hesperian fields,
And o'er the Celtic roamed the utmost isles.

All these and more came flocking; but with looks
Downcast and damp, yet such wherein appeared
Obscure some glimpse of joy, to have found their chief
525 Not in despair, to have found themselves not lost
In loss itself; which on his countenance cast
Like doubtful hue: but he his wonted pride
Soon recollecting, with high words, that bore
Semblance of worth, not substance, gently raised
530 Their fainting courage, and dispelled their fears.
Then straight commands that, at the warlike sound
Of trumpets loud and clarions, be upreared
His mighty standard; that proud honour claimed
Azazel as his right, a cherub tall:
535 Who forthwith from the glittering staff unfurled
Th'imperial ensign, which full high advanced
Shone like a meteor streaming to the wind
With gems and golden lustre rich emblazed,
Seraphic arms and trophies: all the while

540   Sonorous metal blowing martial sounds:
      At which the universal host upsent
      A shout that tore Hell's concave, and beyond
      Frighted the reign of Chaos and old Night.
      All in a moment through the gloom were seen
545   Ten thousand banners rise into the air
      With orient colours waving: with them rose
      A forest huge of spears: and thronging helms
      Appeared, and serried shields in thick array
      Of depth immeasurable: anon they move
550   In perfect phalanx to the Dorian mood
      Of flutes and soft recorders; such as raised
      To highth of noblest temper heroes old
      Arming to battle, and in stead of rage
      Deliberate valour breathed, firm and unmoved
555   With dread of death to flight or foul retreat;
      Nor wanting power to mitigate and swage
      With solemn touches, troubled thoughts, and chase
      Anguish and doubt and fear and sorrow and pain
      From mortal or immortal minds. Thus they
560   Breathing united force with fixèd thought
      Moved on in silence to soft pipes that charmed
      Their painful steps o'er the burnt soil; and now
      Advanced in view they stand, a horrid front
      Of dreadful length and dazzling arms, in guise
565   Of warriors old with ordered spear and shield,
      Awaiting what command their mighty chief
      Had to impose. He through the armed files
      Darts his experienced eye, and soon traverse
      The whole battalion views, their order due,
570   Their visages and stature as of gods,
      Their number last he sums. And now his heart
      Distends with pride, and hardening in his strength
      Glories: for never since created Man,
      Met such embodied force, as named with these

575   Could merit more than that small infantry
        Warred on by cranes: though all the giant brood
        Of Phlegra with th'heroic race were joined
        That fought at Thebes and Ilium, on each side
        Mixed with auxiliar gods; and what resounds
580   In fable or romance of Uther's son
        Begirt with British and Armoric knights;
        And all who since, baptized or infidel
        Jousted in Aspramont or Montalban,
        Damasco, or Marocco, or Trebisond,
585   Or whom Biserta sent from Afric shore
        When Charlemain with all his peerage fell,
        By Fontarabbia.

                Thus far these beyond
        Compare of mortal prowess, yet observed
        Their dread commander: he above the rest
590   In shape and gesture proudly eminent
        Stood like a tower; his form had yet not lost
        All her original brightness, nor appeared
        Less than archangel ruined, and th'excess
        Of glory obscured: as when the sun new risen
595   Looks through the horizontal misty air
        Shorn of his beams, or from behind the moon
        In dim eclipse disastrous twilight sheds
        On half the nations, and with fear of change
        Perplexes monarchs. Darkened so, yet shone
600   Above them all th'archangel: but his face
        Deep scars of thunder had entrenched, and care
        Sat on his faded cheek, but under brows
        Of dauntless courage, and considerate pride
        Waiting revenge: cruel his eye, but cast
605   Signs of remorse and passion to behold
        The fellows of his crime, the followers rather
        (Far other once beheld in bliss) condemned

For ever now to have their lot in pain,
Millions of spirits for his fault amerced
610 Of Heaven, and from eternal splendours flung
For his revolt, yet faithful how they stood,
Their glory withered. As when heaven's fire
Hath scathed the forest oaks, or mountain pines,
With singèd top their stately growth though bare
615 Stands on the blasted heath. He now prepared
To speak; whereat their doubled ranks they bend
From wing to wing, and half enclose him round
With all his peers: attention held them mute.
Thrice he essayed, and thrice in spite of scorn,
620 Tears such as angels weep, burst forth: at last
Words interwove with sighs found out their way.

Satan: 'O myriads of immortal spirits, O powers
Matchless, but with th'Almighty, and that strife
Was not inglorious, though th'event was dire,
625 As this place testifies, and this dire change
Hateful to utter: but what power of mind
Foreseeing or presaging, from the depth
Of knowledge past or present, could have feared,
How such united force of gods, how such
630 As stood like these, could ever know repulse?
For who can yet believe, though after loss,
That all these puissant legions, whose exile
Hath emptied Heaven, shall fail to re-ascend
Self-raised, and repossess their native seat?
635 For me be witness all the host of Heaven,
If counsels different, or danger shunned
By me, have lost our hopes. But he who reigns
Monarch in Heaven, till then as one secure
Sat on his throne, upheld by old repute,
640 Consent or custom, and his regal state
Put forth at full, but still his strength concealed,

Which tempted our attempt, and wrought our fall.
Henceforth his might we know, and know our own
So as not either to provoke, or dread
645 New war, provoked; our better part remains
To work in close design, by fraud or guile
What force effected not: that he no less
At length from us may find, who overcomes
By force, hath overcome but half his foe.
650 Space may produce new worlds; whereof so rife
There went a fame in Heaven that he ere long
Intended to create, and therein plant
A generation, whom his choice regard
Should favour equal to the sons of Heaven:
655 Thither, if but to pry, shall be perhaps
Our first eruption, thither or elsewhere:
For this infernal pit shall never hold
Celestial spirits in bondage, nor th'abyss
Long under darkness cover. But these thoughts
660 Full counsel must mature. Peace is despaired,
For who can think submission? War then, war
Open or understood, must be resolved.'
    He spake: and to confirm his words, out-flew
Millions of flaming swords, drawn from the thighs
665 Of mighty cherubim; the sudden blaze
Far round illumined Hell; highly they raged
Against the Highest, and fierce with graspèd arms
Clashed on their sounding shields the din of war,
Hurling defiance toward the vault of heaven.

670   There stood a hill not far whose grisly top
Belched fire and rolling smoke; the rest entire
Shone with a glossy scurf, undoubted sign
That in his womb was hid metallic ore,
The work of sulphur. Thither winged with speed
675 A numerous brigad hastened. As when bands

Of pioneers with spade and pickaxe armed
Forerun the royal camp, to trench a field,
Or cast a rampart. Mammon led them on,
Mammon, the least erected spirit that fell
680   From Heaven, for even in Heaven his looks and
        thoughts
Were always downward bent, admiring more
The riches of Heaven's pavement, trodden gold,
Than aught divine or holy else enjoyed
In vision beätific: by him first
685   Men also, and by his suggestion taught,
Ransacked the centre, and with impious hands
Rifled the bowels of their mother earth
For treasures better hid. Soon had his crew
Opened into the hill a spacious wound
690   And digged out ribs of gold. Let none admire
That riches grow in Hell; that soil may best
Deserve the precious bane. And here let those
Who boast in mortal things, and wondering tell
Of Babel, and the works of Memphian kings,
695   Learn how their greatest monuments of fame,
And strength and art are easily outdone
By spirits reprobate, and in an hour
What in an age they with incessant toil
And hands innumerable scarce perform.
700   Nigh on the plain in many cells prepared,
That underneath had veins of liquid fire
Sluiced from the lake, a second multitude
With wondrous art founded the massy ore,
Severing each kind, and scummed the bullion dross:
705   A third as soon had formed within the ground
A various mould, and from the boiling cells
By strange conveyance filled each hollow nook,
As in an organ from one blast of wind
To many a row of pipes the sound-board breathes.

710   Anon out of the earth a fabric huge
        Rose like an exhalation, with the sound
        Of dulcet symphonies and voices sweet,
        Built like a temple, where pilasters round
        Were set, and Doric pillars overlaid
715   With golden architrave; nor did there want
        Cornice or frieze, with bossy sculptures graven,
        The roof was fretted gold. Not Babylon,
        Nor great Alcairo such magnificence
        Equalled in all their glories, to enshrine
720   Belus or Serapis their gods, or seat
        Their kings, when Egypt with Assyria strove,
        In wealth and luxury. Th'ascending pile
        Stood fixed her stately highth, and straight the doors
        Opening their brazen folds discover wide
725   Within, her ample spaces, o'er the smooth
        And level pavement: from the archèd roof
        Pendant by subtle magic many a row
        Of starry lamps and blazing cressets fed
        With naphtha and asphaltus yielded light
730   As from a sky. The hasty multitude
        Admiring entered, and the work some praise
        And some the architect: his hand was known
        In Heaven by many a towered structure high,
        Where sceptred angels held their residence,
735   And sat as princes, whom the supreme King
        Exalted to such power, and gave to rule,
        Each in his hierarchy, the orders bright.
        Nor was his name unheard or unadored
        In ancient Greece; and in Ausonian land
740   Men called him Mulciber; and how he fell
        From Heaven, they fabled, thrown by angry Jove
        Sheer o'er the crystal battlements: from morn
        To noon he fell, from noon to dewy eve,
        A summer's day; and with the setting sun

745 Dropped from the zenith like a falling star,
On Lemnos th'Ægean isle: thus they relate,
Erring; for he with this rebellious rout
Fell long before; nor aught availed him now
To have built in Heaven high towers; nor did he scape
750 By all his engines, but was headlong sent
With his industrious crew to build in Hell.

  Meanwhile the wingèd heralds by command
Of sovereign power, with awful ceremony
And trumpets' sound throughout the host proclaim
755 A solemn council forthwith to be held
At Pandæmonium, the high capital
Of Satan and his peers: their summons called
From every band and squarèd regiment
By place or choice the worthiest; they anon
760 With hundreds and with thousands trooping came
Attended: all access was thronged, the gates
And porches wide, but chief the spacious hall
(Though like a covered field, where champions bold
Wont ride in armed, and at the soldan's chair
765 Defied the best of paynim chivalry
To mortal combat or career with lance)
Thick swarmed, both on the ground and in the air,
Brushed with the hiss of rustling wings. As bees
In spring time, when the sun with Taurus rides,
770 Pour forth their populous youth about the hive
In clusters; they among fresh dews and flowers
Fly to and fro, or on the smoothèd plank,
The suburb of their straw-built citadel,
New rubbed with balm, expatiate and confer
775 Their state affairs. So thick the airy crowd
Swarmed and were straitened; till the signal given,
Behold a wonder! they but now who seemed
In bigness to surpass Earth's giant sons

Now less than smallest dwarfs, in narrow room
780 Throng numberless, like that pygmean race
Beyond the Indian mount, or fairy elves,
Whose midnight revels, by a forest side
Or fountain some belated peasant sees,
Or dreams he sees, while overhead the moon
785 Sits arbitress, and nearer to the Earth
Wheels her pale course, they on their mirth and dance
Intent, with jocund music charm his ear;
At once with joy and fear his heart rebounds.
Thus incorporeal spirits to smallest forms
790 Reduced their shapes immense, and were at large,
Though without number still amidst the hall
Of that infernal court. But far within
And in their own dimensions like themselves
The great seraphic lords and cherubim
795 In close recess and secret conclave sat
A thousand demi-gods on golden seats,
Frequent and full. After short silence then
And summons read, the great consult began.

Book II

High on a throne of royal state, which far
Outshone the wealth of Ormus and of Ind,
Or where the gorgeous East with richest hand
Showers on her kings barbaric pearl and gold,
5   Satan exalted sat, by merit raised
To that bad eminence; and from despair
Thus high uplifted beyond hope, aspires
Beyond thus high, insatiate to pursue
Vain war with Heaven, and by success untaught
10   His proud imaginations thus displayed.
Satan: 'Powers and Dominions, deities of heaven,
For since no deep within her gulf can hold
Immortal vigour, though oppressed and fallen,
I give not Heaven for lost. From this descent
15   Celestial virtues rising, will appear
More glorious and more dread than from no fall,
And trust themselves to fear no second fate:
Me though just right, and the fixed laws of Heaven
Did first create your leader, next, free choice,
20   With what besides, in counsel or in fight,
Hath been achieved of merit, yet this loss
Thus far at least recovered, hath much more
Established in a safe unenvied throne
Yielded with full consent. The happier state
25   In Heaven, which follows dignity, might draw
Envy from each inferior; but who here
Will envy whom the highest place exposes
Foremost to stand against the Thunderer's aim
Your bulwark, and condemns to greatest share
30   Of endless pain? where there is then no good
For which to strive, no strife can grow up there

From faction; for none sure will claim in Hell
Precédence, none, whose portion is so small
Of present pain, that with ambitious mind
35   Will covet more. With this advantage then
To union, and firm faith, and firm accord,
More than can be in Heaven, we now return
To claim our just inheritance of old,
Surer to prosper than prosperity
40   Could have assured us; and by what best way,
Whether of open war or covert guile,
We now debate; who can advise, may speak.'

He ceased, and next him Moloch, sceptered king
Stood up, the strongest and the fiercest spirit
45   That fought in Heaven; now fiercer by despair:
His trust was with th'Eternal to be deemed
Equal in strength, and rather than be less
Cared not to be at all; with that care lost
Went all his fear: of God, or Hell, or worse
50   He recked not, and these words thereafter spake.
Moloch: 'My sentence is for open war: of wiles,
More unexpert, I boast not: them let those
Contrive who need, or when they need, not now.
For while they sit contriving, shall the rest,
55   Millions that stand in arms, and longing wait
The signal to ascend, sit lingering here
Heaven's fugitives, and for their dwelling place
Accept this dark opprobrious den of shame,
The prison of his tyranny who reigns
60   By our delay? no, let us rather choose
Armed with Hell flames and fury all at once
O'er Heaven's high towers to force resistless way,
Turning our tortures into horrid arms
Against the Torturer; when to meet the noise
65   Of his almighty engine he shall hear

Infernal thunder, and for lightning see
Black fire and horror shot with equal rage
Among his angels; and his throne itself
Mixed with Tartarean sulphur, and strange fire,
70   His own invented torments. But perhaps
The way seems difficult and steep to scale
With upright wing against a higher foe.
Let such bethink them, if the sleepy drench
Of that forgetful lake benumb not still,
75   That in our proper motion we ascend
Up to our native seat: descent and fall
To us is adverse. Who but felt of late
When the fierce foe hung on our broken rear
Insulting, and pursued us through the deep,
80   With what compulsion and laborious flight
We sunk thus low? Th'ascent is easy then;
Th'event is feared; should we again provoke
Our Stronger, some worse way his wrath may find
To our destruction: if there be in Hell
85   Fear to be worse destroyed: what can be worse
Than to dwell here, driven out from bliss, condemned
In this abhorrèd deep to utter woe;
Where pain of unextinguishable fire
Must exercise us without hope of end
90   The vassals of his anger, when the scourge
Inexorably, and the torturing hour
Call us to penance? More destroyed than thus
We should be quite abolished and expire.
What fear we then? what doubt we to incense
95   His utmost ire? which to the highth enraged,
Will either quite consume us, and reduce
To nothing this essential, happier far
Than miserable to have eternal being:
Or if our substance be indeed divine,
100   And cannot cease to be, we are at worst

On this side nothing; and by proof we feel
Our power sufficient to disturb his Heaven,
And with perpetual inroads to alarm,
Though inaccessible, his fatal throne:
105 Which if not victory is yet revenge.'

He ended frowning, and his look denounced
Desperate revenge, and battle dangerous
To less than gods. On th'other side up rose
Belial, in act more graceful and humane;
110 A fairer person lost not Heaven; he seemed
For dignity composed and high exploit:
But all was false and hollow; though his tongue
Dropped manna, and could make the worse appear
The better reason, to perplex and dash
115 Maturest counsels: for his thoughts were low;
To vice industrious, but to nobler deeds
Timorous and slothful: yet he pleased the ear,
And with persuasive accent thus began.
Belial: 'I should be much for open war, O peers,
120 As not behind in hate; if what was urged
Main reason to persuade immediate war,
Did not dissuade me most, and seem to cast
Ominous conjecture on the whole success:
When he who most excels in fact of arms,
125 In what he counsels and in what excels
Mistrustful, grounds his courage on despair
And utter dissolution, as the scope
Of all his aim, after some dire revenge.
First, what revenge? The towers of Heaven are filled
130 With armèd watch, that render all access
Impregnable; oft on the bordering deep
Encamp their legions, or with óbscure wing
Scout far and wide into the realm of Night,
Scorning surprise. Or could we break our way

135   By force, and at our heels all Hell should rise
        With blackest insurrection, to confound
        Heaven's purest light, yet our great Enemy
        All incorruptible would on his throne
        Sit unpolluted, and th'ethereal mould
140   Incapable of stain would soon expel
        Her mischief, and purge off the baser fire
        Victorious. Thus repulsed, our final hope
        Is flat despair: we must exasperate
        Th'almighty Victor to spend all his rage,
145   And that must end us, that must be our cure,
        To be no more; sad cure; for who would lose,
        Though full of pain, this intellectual being,
        Those thoughts that wander through eternity,
        To perish rather, swallowed up and lost
150   In the wide womb of uncreated night,
        Devoid of sense and motion? and who knows,
        Let this be good, whether our angry Foe
        Can give it, or will ever? how he can
        Is doubtful; that he never will is sure.
155   Will he, so wise, let loose at once his ire,
        Belike through impotence, or unaware,
        To give his enemies their wish, and end
        Them in his anger, whom his anger saves
        To punish endless? wherefore cease we then?
160   Say they who counsel war, we are decreed,
        Reserved and destined to eternal woe;
        Whatever doing, what can we suffer more,
        What can we suffer worse? is this then worst,
        Thus sitting, thus consulting, thus in arms?
165   What when we fled amain, pursued and strook
        With Heaven's afflicting thunder, and besought
        The deep to shelter us? this Hell then seemed
        A refuge from those wounds: or when we lay
        Chained on the burning lake? that sure was worse.

170 What if the breath that kindled those grim fires
Awaked should blow them into sevenfold rage
And plunge us in the flames? or from above
Should intermitted vengeance arm again
His red right hand to plague us? what if all
175 Her stores were opened, and this firmament
Of Hell should spout her cataracts of fire,
Impendent horrors, threatening hideous fall
One day upon our heads; while we perhaps
Designing or exhorting glorious war,
180 Caught in a fiery tempest shall be hurled
Each on his rock transfixed, the sport and prey
Of racking whirlwinds, or for ever sunk
Under yon boiling ocean, wrapped in chains;
There to converse with everlasting groans,
185 Unrespited, unpitied, unreprieved,
Ages of hopeless end; this would be worse.
War therefore, open or concealed, alike
My voice dissuades; for what can force or guile
With him, or who deceive his mind, whose eye
190 Views all things at one view? he from Heaven's highth
All these our motions vain, sees and derides;
Not more almighty to resist our might
Than wise to frústrate all our plots and wiles.
Shall we then live thus vile, the race of Heaven
195 Thus trampled, thus expelled to suffer here
Chains and these torments? Better these than worse
By my advice; since fate inevitable
Subdues us, and omnipotent decree,
The Victor's will. To suffer, as to do,
200 Our strength is equal, nor the law unjust
That so ordains: this was at first resolved,
If we were wise, against so great a Foe
Contending, and so doubtful what might fall.
I laugh, when those who at the spear are bold

205   And venturous, if that fail them, shrink and fear
       What yet they know must follow, to endure
       Exile, or ignominy, or bonds, or pain,
       The sentence of their conqueror. This is now
       Our doom; which if we can sustain and bear,
210   Our súpreme Foe in time may much remit
       His anger, and perhaps thus far removed
       Not mind us not offending, satisfied
       With what is punished; whence these raging fires
       Will slacken, if his breath stir not their flames.
215   Our purer essence then will overcome
       Their noxious vapour, or inured not feel,
       Or changed at length, and to the place conformed
       In temper and in nature, will receive
       Familiar the fierce heat, and void of pain;
220   This horror will grow mild, this darkness light,
       Besides what hope the never-ending flight
       Of future days may bring, what chance, what change
       Worth waiting, since our present lot appears
       For happy though but ill, for ill not worst,
225   If we procure not to ourselves more woe.'
         Thus Belial with words clothed in reason's garb
       Counselled ignoble ease, and peaceful sloth,
       Not peace: and after him thus Mammon spake.

Mammon: 'Either to disenthrone the King of Heaven
230   We war, if war be best, or to regain
       Our own right lost: him to unthrone we then
       May hope when everlasting fate shall yield
       To fickle chance, and Chaos judge the strife:
       The former vain to hope argues as vain
235   The latter: for what place can be for us
       Within Heaven's bound, unless Heaven's Lord
          supreme
       We overpower? Suppose he should relent

And publish grace to all, on promise made
Of new subjection; with what eyes could we
240   Stand in his presence humble, and receive
Strict laws imposed, to celebrate his throne
With warbled hymns, and to his Godhead sing
Forced hallelujahs? while he lordly sits
Our envied Sovereign, and his altar breathes
245   Ambrosial odours and ambrosial flowers,
Our servile offerings. This must be our task
In Heaven, this our delight; how wearisome
Eternity so spent in worship paid
To whom we hate. Let us not then pursue
250   By force impossible, by leave obtained
Unacceptable, though in Heaven, our state
Of splendid vassalage, but rather seek
Our own good from ourselves, and from our own
Live to ourselves, though in this vast recess,
255   Free, and to none accountable, preferring
Hard liberty before the easy yoke
Of servile pomp. Our greatness will appear
Then most conspicuous, when great things of small,
Useful of hurtful, prosperous of adverse
260   We can create, and in what place so e'er
Thrive under evil, and work ease out of pain
Through labour and endurance. This deep world
Of darkness do we dread? How oft amidst
Thick clouds and dark doth Heaven's all-ruling Sire
265   Choose to reside, his glory unobscured,
And with the majesty of darkness round
Covers his throne; from whence deep thunders roar
Mustering their rage, and Heaven resembles Hell?
As he our darkness, cannot we his light
270   Imitate when we please? This desert soil
Wants not her hidden lustre, gems and gold;
Nor want we skill or art, from whence to raise

Magnificence; and what can Heaven show more?
Our torments also may in length of time
275   Become our elements, these piercing fires
As soft as now severe, our temper changed
Into their temper; which must needs remove
The sensible of pain. All things invite
To peaceful counsels, and the settled state
280   Of order, how in safety best we may
Compose our present evils, with regard
Of what we are and where, dismissing quite
All thoughts of war: ye have what I advise.'

He scarce had finished, when such murmur filled
285   Th'assembly, as when hollow rocks retain
The sound of blust'ring winds, which all night long
Had roused the sea, now with hoarse cadence lull
Seafaring men o'erwatched, whose bark by chance
Or pinnace anchors in a craggy bay
290   After the tempest: such applause was heard
As Mammon ended, and his sentence pleased,
Advising peace: for such another field
They dreaded worse than Hell: so much the fear
Of thunder and the sword of Michaël
295   Wrought still within them; and no less desire
To found this nether empire, which might rise
By policy, and long process of time,
In emulation opposite to Heaven.
Which when Beëlzebub perceived, than whom,
300   Satan except, none higher sat, with grave
Aspect he rose, and in his rising seemed
A pillar of state; deep on his front engraven
Deliberation sat and public care;
And princely counsel in his face yet shone,
305   Majestic though in ruin: sage he stood
With Atlantean shoulders fit to bear

The weight of mightiest monarchies; his look
Drew audience and attention still as night
Or summer's noontide air, while thus he spake.

310 **Beëlzebub:** 'Thrones and imperial powers, offspring of
Heaven,
Ethereal virtues; or these titles now
Must we renounce, and changing style be called
Princes of Hell? for so the popular vote
Inclines, here to continue, and build up here
315 A growing empire; doubtless; while we dream,
And know not that the King of Heaven hath doomed
This place our dungeon, not our safe retreat
Beyond his potent arm, to live exempt
From Heaven's high jurisdiction, in new league
320 Banded against his throne, but to remain
In strictest bondage, though thus far removed,
Under th'inevitable curb, reserved
His captive multitude: for he, be sure,
In highth or depth, still first and last will reign
325 Sole King, and of his kingdom lose no part
By our revolt, but over Hell extend
His empire, and with iron sceptre rule
Us here, as with his golden those in Heaven.
What sit we then projecting peace and war?
330 War hath determined us, and foiled with loss
Irreparable; terms of peace yet none
Vouchsafed or sought; for what peace will be given
To us enslaved, but custody severe,
And stripes, and arbitrary punishment
335 Inflicted? and what peace can we return,
But to our power hostility and hate,
Untamed reluctance, and revenge though slow,
Yet ever plotting how the Conqueror least
May reap his conquest, and may least rejoice

340   In doing what we most in suffering feel?
        Nor will occasion want, nor shall we need
        With dangerous expedition to invade
        Heaven, whose high walls fear no assault or siege,
        Or ambush from the deep. What if we find
345   Some easier enterprise? There is a place
        (If ancient and prophetic fame in Heaven
        Err not) another world, the happy seat
        Of some new race called Man, about this time
        To be created like to us, though less
350   In power and excellence, but favoured more
        Of him who rules above; so was his will
        Pronounced among the gods, and by an oath,
        That shook Heaven's whole circumference,
              confirmed.
        Thither let us bend all our thoughts, to learn
355   What creatures there inhabit, of what mould,
        Or substance, how endued, and what their power,
        And where their weakness, how attempted best,
        By force or subtlety. Though Heaven be shut,
        And Heaven's high Arbitrator sit secure
360   In his own strength, this place may lie exposed
        The utmost border of his kingdom, left
        To their defence who hold it: here perhaps
        Some advantageous act may be achieved
        By sudden onset, either with Hell fire
365   To waste his whole creation, or possess
        All as our own, and drive as we were driven,
        The puny habitants, or if not drive,
        Seduce them to our party, that their God
        May prove their foe, and with repenting hand
370   Abolish his own works. This would surpass
        Common revenge, and interrupt his joy
        In our confusion, and our joy upraise
        In his disturbance; when his darling sons

Hurled headlong to partake with us, shall curse
375   Their frail originals and faded bliss,
Faded so soon. Advise if this be worth
Attempting, or to sit in darkness here
Hatching vain empires?' Thus Beëlzebub
Pleaded his devilish counsel, first devised
380   By Satan, and in part proposed: for whence,
But from the author of all ill could spring
So deep a malice, to confound the race
Of Mankind in one root, and Earth with Hell
To mingle and involve, done all to spite
385   The great Creator? But their spite still serves
His glory to augment. The bold design
Pleased highly those infernal states, and joy
Sparkled in all their eyes; with full assent
They vote: whereat his speech he thus renews.

390 **Beëlzebub:** 'Well have ye judged, well ended long debate,
Synod of gods, and like to what ye are,
Great things resolved; which from the lowest deep
Will once more lift us up, in spite of fate,
Nearer our ancient seat; perhaps in view
395   Of those bright confines, whence with neighbouring
        arms
And opportune excursion we may chance
Re-enter Heaven; or else in some mild zone
Dwell not unvisited of Heaven's fair light
Secure, and at the brightening orient beam
400   Purge off this gloom; the soft delicious air,
To heal the scar of these corrosive fires
Shall breathe her balm. But first whom shall we send
In search of this new world, whom shall we find
Sufficient? who shall tempt with wandering feet
405   The dark unbottomed infinite abyss
And through the palpable obscure find out

His uncouth way, or spread his airy flight
Upborne with indefatigable wings
Over the vast abrupt, ere he arrive
410   The happy isle; what strength, what art can then
Suffice, or what evasion bear him safe
Through the strict sentries and stations thick
Of angels watching round? Here he had need
All circumspection, and we now no less
415   Choice in our suffrage; for on whom we send,
The weight of all and our last hope relies.'
    This said, he sat; and expectation held
His look suspense, awaiting who appeared
To second, or oppose, or undertake
420   The perilous attempt: but all sat mute,
Pondering the danger with deep thoughts; and each
In other's countenance read his own dismay
Astonished: none among the choice and prime
Of those Heaven-warring champions could be found
425   So hardy as to proffer or accept
Alone the dreadful voyage; till at last
Satan, whom now transcendent glory raised
Above his fellows, with monarchal pride
Conscious of highest worth, unmoved thus spake.

430 **Satan:** 'O progeny of heaven, empyreal thrones,
With reason hath deep silence and demur
Seized us, though undismayed: long is the way
And hard, that out of Hell leads up to light;
Our prison strong, this huge convex of fire,
435   Outrageous to devour, immures us round
Ninefold, and gates of burning adamant
Barred over us prohibit all egress.
These passed, if any pass, the void profound
Of unessential night receives him next
440   Wide gaping, and with utter loss of being

Threatens him, plunged in that abortive gulf.
If thence he scape into whatever world,
Or unknown region, what remains him less,
Than unknown dangers and as hard escape?
445 But I should ill become this throne, O peers,
And this imperial sovereignty, adorned
With splendour, armed with power, if aught proposed
And judged of public moment, in the shape
Of difficulty or danger could deter
450 Me from attempting. Wherefore do I assume
These royalties, and not refuse to reign,
Refusing to accept as great a share
Of hazard as of honour, due alike
To him who reigns, and so much to him due
455 Of hazard more, as he above the rest
High honoured sits? Go therefore mighty powers,
Terror of Heaven, though fallen; intend at home,
While here shall be our home, what best may ease
The present misery, and render Hell
460 More tolerable; if there be cure or charm
To respite or deceive, or slack the pain
Of this ill mansion: intermit no watch
Against a wakeful foe, while I abroad
Through all the coasts of dark destruction seek
465 Deliverance for us all: this enterprise
None shall partake with me.'

                                      Thus saying rose
The monarch, and prevented all reply,
Prudent, lest from his resolution raised
Others among the chief might offer now
470 (Certain to be refused) what erst they feared;
And so refused might in opinion stand
His rivals, winning cheap the high repute
Which he through hazard huge must earn. But they

Dreaded not more th'adventure than his voice
475 Forbidding; and at once with him they rose;
Their rising all at once was as the sound
Of thunder heard remote. Towards him they bend
With awful reference prone; and as a god
Extol him equal to the highest in Heaven:
480 Nor failed they to express how much they praised,
That for the general safety he despised
His own: for neither do the spirits damned
Lose all their virtue; lest bad men should boast
Their specious deeds on earth, which glory excites,
485 Or close ambition varnished o'er with zeal.
Thus they their doubtful consultations dark
Ended rejoicing in their matchless chief:
As when from mountain tops the dusky clouds
Ascending, while the north wind sleeps, o'erspread
490 Heaven's cheerful face, the louring element
Scowls o'er the darkened landskip snow, or shower;
If chance the radiant sun with farewell sweet
Extend his evening beam, the fields revive,
The birds their notes renew, and bleating herds
495 Attest their joy, that hill and valley rings.
O shame to men! Devil with devil damned
Firm concord holds, men only disagree
Of creatures rational, though under hope
Of heavenly grace: and God proclaiming peace,
500 Yet live in hatred, enmity, and strife
Among themselves, and levy cruel wars,
Wasting the earth, each other to destroy:
As if (which might induce us to accord)
Man had not hellish foes enow besides,
505 That day and night for his destruction wait.

The Stygian council thus dissolved; and forth
In order came the grand infernal peers,

Midst came their mighty paramount, and seemed
Alone the antagonist of Heaven, nor less
510 Than Hell's dread emperor with pomp supreme,
And God-like imitated state; him round
A globe of fiery seraphim enclosed
With bright emblazonry, and horrent arms.
Then of their session ended they bid cry
515 With trumpets' regal sound the great result:
Toward the four winds four speedy cherubim
Put to their mouths the sounding alchemy
By herald's voice explained: the hollow abyss
Heard far and wide, and all the host of Hell
520 With deafening shout returned them loud acclaim.
Thence more at ease their minds and somewhat raised
By false presumptuous hope, the rangèd powers
Disband, and wandering, each his several way
Pursues, as inclination or sad choice
525 Leads him perplexed, where he may likeliest find
Truce to his restless thoughts, and entertain
The irksome hours, till his great chief return.
Part on the plain, or in the air sublime
Upon the wing, or in swift race contend,
530 As at th'Olympian games or Pythian fields;
Part curb their fiery steeds, or shun the goal
With rapid wheels, or fronted brigads form.
As when to warn proud cities war appears
Waged in the troubled sky, and armies rush
535 To battle in the clouds, before each van
Prick forth the airy knights, and couch their spears
Till thickest legions close; with feats of arms
From either end of heaven the welkin burns.
Others with vast Typhœan rage more fell
540 Rend up both rocks and hills, and ride the air
In whirlwind; Hell scarce holds the wild uproar.
As when Alcides from Oechalia crowned

With conquest, felt th'envenomed robe, and tore
Through pain up by the roots Thessalian pines,
545 And Lichas from the top of Oeta threw
Into the Euboic sea. Others more mild,
Retreated in a silent valley, sing
With notes angelical to many a harp
Their own heroic deeds and hapless fall
550 By doom of battle; and complain that fate
Free virtue should enthral to force or chance.
Their song was partial, but the harmony
(What could it less when spirits immortal sing?)
Suspended Hell, and took with ravishment
555 The thronging audience. In discóurse more sweet
(For eloquence the soul, song charms the sense)
Others apart sat on a hill retired,
In thoughts more elevate, and reasoned high
Of providence, foreknowledge, will, and fate,
560 Fixed fate, free will, foreknowledge absolute,
And found no end, in wandering mazes lost.
Of good and evil much they argued then,
Of happiness and final misery,
Passion and apathy, and glory and shame,
565 Vain wisdom all, and false philosophy:
Yet with a pleasing sorcery could charm
Pain for a while or anguish, and excite
Fallacious hope, or arm th'obdurèd breast
With stubborn patience as with triple steel.

570 Another part in squadrons and gross bands,
On bold adventure to discover wide
That dismal world, if any clime perhaps
Might yield them easier habitation, bend
Four ways their flying march, along the banks
575 Of four infernal rivers that disgorge
Into the burning lake their baleful streams;

Abhorrèd Styx the flood of deadly hate,
Sad Acheron of sorrow, black and deep;
Cocytus, named of lamentation loud
580   Heard on the rueful stream; fierce Phlegethon
Whose waves of torrent fire inflame with rage.
Far off from these a slow and silent stream,
Lethè the river of oblivion rolls
Her watery labyrinth, whereof who drinks,
585   Forthwith his former state and being forgets,
Forgets both joy and grief, pleasure and pain.
Beyond this flood a frozen continent
Lies dark and wild, beat with perpetual storms
Of whirlwind and dire hail, which on firm land
590   Thaws not, but gathers heap, and ruin seems
Of ancient pile; all else deep snow and ice,
A gulf profound as that Serbonian bog
Betwixt Damiata and Mount Casius old,
Where armies whole have sunk: the parching air
595   Burns frore, and cold performs th'effect of fire.
Thither by harpy-footed Furies haled,
At certain revolutions all the damned
Are brought: and feel by turns the bitter change
Of fierce extremes, extremes by change more fierce,
600   From beds of raging fire to starve in ice
Their soft ethereal warmth, and there to pine
Immovable, infixed, and frozen round,
Periods of time, thence hurried back to fire.
They ferry over this Lethean sound
605   Both to and fro, their sorrow to augment,
And wish and struggle, as they pass, to reach
The tempting stream, with one small drop to lose
In sweet forgetfulness all pain and woe,
All in one moment, and so near the brink;
610   But fate withstands, and to oppose th'attempt
Medusa with Gorgonian terror guards

The ford, and of itself the water flies
All taste of living wight, as once it fled
The lip of Tantalus. Thus roving on
615 In confused march forlorn, th'adventurous bands
With shuddering horror pale, and eyes aghast
Viewed first their lámentable lot, and found
No rest: through many a dark and dreary vale
They passed, and many a region dolorous,
620 O'er many a frozen, many a fiery alp,
Rocks, caves, lakes, fens, bogs, dens, and shades of
        death,
A universe of death, which God by curse
Created evil, for evil only good,
Where all life dies, death lives, and nature breeds,
625 Perverse, all monstrous, all prodigious things,
Abominable, inutterable, and worse
Than fables yet have feigned, or fear conceived,
Gorgons and Hydras, and Chimèras dire.

Meanwhile the adversary of God and Man,
630 Satan with thoughts inflamed of highest design,
Puts on swift wings, and towards the gates of Hell
Explores his solitary flight; sometimes
He scours the right hand coast, sometimes the left,
Now shaves with level wing the deep, then soars
635 Up to the fiery concave touring high.
As when far off at sea a fleet descried
Hangs in the clouds, by equinoctial winds
Close sailing from Bengala, or the isles
Of Ternate and Tidore, whence merchants bring
640 Their spicy drugs: they on the trading flood
Through the wide Ethiopian to the Cape
Ply stemming nightly toward the pole. So seemed
Far off the flying fiend: at last appear
Hell bounds high reaching to the horrid roof,

645 And thrice threefold the gates; three folds were brass,
Three irön, three of adamantine rock,
Impenetrable, impaled with circling fire,
Yet unconsumed. Before the gates there sat
On either side a formidable shape;
650 The one seemed woman to the waist, and fair,
But ended foul in many a scaly fold
Voluminous and vast, a serpent armed
With mortal sting: about her middle round
A cry of Hell hounds never ceasing barked
655 With wide Cerberean mouths full loud, and rung
A hideous peal: yet, when they list, would creep,
If aught disturbed their noise, into her womb,
And kennel there, yet there still barked and howled
Within unseen. Far less abhorred than these
660 Vexed Scylla bathing in the sea that parts
Calabria from the hoarse Trinacrian shore:
Nor uglier follow the night-hag, when called
In secret, riding through the air she comes
Lured with the smell of infant blood, to dance
665 With Lapland witches, while the labouring moon
Eclipses at their charms. The other shape,
If shape it might be called that shape had none
Distinguishable in member, joint, or limb,
Or substance might be called that shadow seemed,
670 For each seemed either; black it stood as night,
Fierce as ten Furies, terrible as Hell,
And shook a dreadful dart; what seemed his head
The likeness of a kingly crown had on.
Satan was now at hand, and from his seat
675 The monster moving onwards came as fast
With horrid strides, Hell trembled as he strode.
Th'undaunted fiend what this might be admired,
Admired, not feared; God and his Son except,
Created thing nought valued he nor shunned;

680   And with disdainful look thus first began.

Satan: 'Whence and what art thou, execrable shape,
          That dar'st, though grim and terrible, advance
          Thy miscreated front athwart my way
          To yonder gates? through them I mean to pass,
685   That be assured, without leave asked of thee:
          Retire, or taste thy folly, and learn by proof,
          Hell-born, not to contend with spirits of Heaven.'
              To whom the goblin full of wrath replied,
Death: 'Art thou that traitor angel, art thou he,
690   Who first broke peace in Heaven and faith, till then
          Unbroken, and in proud rebellious arms
          Drew after him the third part of Heaven's sons
          Conjured against the Highest, for which both thou
          And they outcast from God, are here condemned
695   To waste eternal days in woe and pain?
          And reckon'st thou thyself with spirits of Heaven,
          Hell-doomed, and breath'st defiance here and scorn
          Where I reign king, and to enrage thee more,
          Thy king and lord? Back to thy punishment,
700   False fugitive, and to thy speed add wings,
          Lest with a whip of scorpions I pursue
          Thy lingering, or with one stroke of this dart
          Strange horror seize thee, and pangs unfelt before.'
              So spake the grisly terror, and in shape,
705   So speaking and so threatening, grew tenfold
          More dreadful and deform: on th'other side
          Incensed with indignation Satan stood
          Unterrified, and like a comet burned,
          That fires the length of Ophiucus huge
710   In th'arctic sky, and from his horrid hair
          Shakes pestilence and war. Each at the head
          Levelled his deadly aim; their fatal hands
          No second stroke intend, and such a frown

Each cast at th'other, as when two black clouds
715 With heaven's artillery fraught, come rattling on
Over the Caspian, then stand front to front
Hovering a space, till winds the signal blow
To join their dark encounter in mid air:
So frowned the mighty combatants, that Hell
720 Grew darker at their frown, so matched they stood;
For never but once more was either like
To meet so great a foe: and now great deeds
Had been achieved, whereof all Hell had rung,
Had not the snaky sorceress that sat
725 Fast by Hell gate, and kept the fatal key,
Risen, and with hideous outcry rushed between.
Sin: 'O father, what intends thy hand,' she cried,
'Against thy only son? What fury, O son,
Possesses thee to bend that mortal dart
730 Against thy father's head? and know'st for whom?
For him who sits above and laughs the while
At thee ordained his drudge, to execute
Whate'er his wrath, which he calls justice, bids,
His wrath which one day will destroy ye both.'
735 She spake, and at her words the hellish pest
Forbore, then these to her Satan returned:
Satan: 'So strange thy outcry, and thy words so strange
Thou interposest, that my sudden hand
Prevented spares to tell thee yet by deeds
740 What it intends; till first I know of thee,
What thing thou art, thus double-formed, and why
In this infernal vale first met thou call'st
Me father, and that phantasm call'st my son?
I know thee not, nor ever saw till now
745 Sight more detestable than him and thee.'

T'whom thus the portress of Hell gate replied:
Sin: 'Hast thou forgot me then, and do I seem

Now in thine eye so foul, once deemed so fair
In Heaven, when at the assembly, and in sight
750 Of all the seraphim with thee combined
In bold conspiracy against Heaven's King,
All on a sudden miserable pain
Surprised thee, dim thine eyes, and dizzy swum
In darkness, while thy head flames thick and fast
755 Threw forth, till on the left side opening wide,
Likest to thee in shape and countenance bright,
Then shining heavenly fair, a goddess armed
Out of thy head I sprung: amazement seized
All th'host of Heaven; back they recoiled afraid
760 At first, and called me Sin, and for a sign
Portentous held me; but familiar grown,
I pleased, and with attractive graces won
The most averse, thee chiefly, who full oft
Thyself in me thy perfect image viewing
765 Becam'st enamoured, and such joy thou took'st
With me in secret, that my womb conceived
A growing burden. Meanwhile war arose,
And fields were fought in heaven; wherein remained
(For what could else) to our almighty Foe
770 Clear victory, to our part loss and rout
Through all th'Empyrean: down they fell
Driven headlong from the pitch of Heaven, down
Into this deep, and in the general fall
I also; at which time this powerful key
775 Into my hand was given, with charge to keep
These gates for ever shut, which none can pass
Without my opening. Pensive here I sat
Alone, but long I sat not, till my womb
Pregnant by thee, and now excessive grown
780 Prodigious motion felt and rueful throes.
At last this odious offspring whom thou seest
Thine own begotten, breaking violent way

Tore through my entrails, that with fear and pain
Distorted, all my nether shape thus grew
785   Transformed: but he my inbred enemy
Forth issued, brandishing his fatal dart
Made to destroy: I fled, and cried out 'Death';
Hell trembled at the hideous name, and sighed
From all her caves, and back resounded 'Death'.
790   I fled, but he pursued (though more, it seems,
Inflamed with lust than rage) and swifter far,
Me overtook his mother all dismayed,
And in embraces forcible and foul
Ingendering with me, of that rape begot
795   These yelling monsters that with ceaseless cry
Surround me, as thou saw'st, hourly conceived
And hourly born, with sorrow infinite
To me, for when they list into the womb
That bred them they return, and howl and gnaw
800   My bowels, their repast; then bursting forth
Afresh with conscious terrors vex me round,
That rest or intermission none I find.
Before mine eyes in opposition sits
Grim Death my son and foe, who sets them on,
805   And me his parent would full soon devour
For want of other prey, but that he knows
His end with mine involved; and knows that I
Should prove a bitter morsel, and his bane,
Whenever that shall be; so fate pronounced.
810   But thou, O father, I forewarn thee, shun
His deadly arrow; neither vainly hope
To be invulnerable in those bright arms,
Though tempered heavenly, for that mortal dint,
Save he who reigns above, none can resist.'

815   She finished, and the subtle fiend his lore
Soon learned, now milder, and thus answered smooth.

Satan: 'Dear daughter, since thou claim'st me for thy sire,
And my fair son here show'st me, the dear pledge
Of dalliance had with thee in Heaven, and joys
820   Then sweet, now sad to mention, through dire change
Befallen us unforeseen, unthought of, know
I come no enemy, but to set free
From out this dark and dismal house of pain,
Both him and thee, and all the heavenly host
825   Of spirits that in our just pretences armed
Fell with us from on high: from them I go
This uncouth errand sole, and one for all
Myself expose, with lonely steps to tread
Th'unfounded deep, and through the void immense
830   To search with wandering quest a place foretold
Should be, and, by concurring signs, ere now
Created vast and round, a place of bliss
In the purlieus of Heaven, and therein placed
A race of upstart creatures, to supply
835   Perhaps our vacant room, though more removed,
Lest Heaven surcharged with potent multitude
Might hap to move new broils. Be this or aught
Than this more secret now designed, I haste
To know, and this once known, shall soon return,
840   And bring ye to the place where thou and Death
Shall dwell at ease, and up and down unseen
Wing silently the buxom air, embalmed
With odours; there ye shall be fed and filled
Immeasurably, all things shall be your prey.'
845   He ceased, for both seemed highly pleased, and Death
Grinned horrible a ghastly smile, to hear
His famine should be filled, and blessed his maw
Destined to that good hour: no less rejoiced
His mother bad, and thus bespake her sire.
850   **Sin:**   'The key of this infernal pit by due,
And by command of Heaven's all-powerful King

I keep, by him forbidden to unlock
These adamantine gates; against all force
Death ready stands to interpose his dart,
855 Fearless to be o'ermatched by living might.
But what owe I to his commands above
Who hates me, and hath hither thrust me down
Into this gloom of Tartarus profound,
To sit in hateful office here confined,
860 Inhabitant of Heaven, and heavenly-born,
Here in perpetual agony and pain,
With terrors and with clamours compassed round
Of mine own brood, that on my bowels feed?
Thou art my father, thou my author, thou
865 My being gav'st me; whom should I obey
But thee, whom follow? thou wilt bring me soon
To that new world of light and bliss, among
The gods who live at ease, where I shall reign
At thy right hand voluptuous, as beseems
870 Thy daughter and thy darling, without end.'
    Thus saying, from her side the fatal key,
Sad instrument of all our woe, she took;
And towards the gate rolling her bestial train,
Forthwith the huge portcullis high updrew,
875 Which but herself not all the Stygian powers
Could once have moved; then in the key-hole turns
The intricate wards, and every bolt and bar
Of massy iron or solid rock with ease
Unfastens: on a sudden open fly
880 With impetuous recoil and jarring sound
The infernal doors, and on their hinges grate
Harsh thunder, that the lowest bottom shook
Of Érebus. She opened, but to shut
Excelled her power; the gates wide open stood,
885 That with extended wings a bannered host
Under spread ensigns marching might pass through

With horse and chariots ranked in loose array;
So wide they stood, and like a furnace mouth
Cast forth redounding smoke and ruddy flame.

890 Before their eyes in sudden view appear
The secrets of the hoary deep, a dark
Illimitable ocean without bound,
Without dimension, where length, breadth, and
    highth,
And time and place are lost; where eldest Night
895 And Chaos, ancestors of Nature, hold
Eternal anarchy, amidst the noise
Of endless wars, and by confusion stand.
For hot, cold, moist, and dry, four champions fierce
Strive here for mastery, and to battle bring
900 Their embryon atoms; they around the flag
Of each his faction, in their several clans,
Light-armed or heavy, sharp, smooth, swift or slow,
Swarm populous, unnumbered as the sands
Of Barca or Cyrenè's torrid soil,
905 Levied to side with warring winds, and poise
Their lighter wings. To whom these most adhere,
He rules a moment; Chaos umpire sits,
And by decision more embroils the fray
By which he reigns: next him high arbiter
910 Chance governs all. Into this wild abyss,
The womb of Nature and perhaps her grave,
Of neither sea, nor shore, nor air, nor fire,
But all these in their pregnant causes mixed
Confusedly, and which thus must ever fight,
915 Unless th'Almighty Maker them ordain
His dark materials to create more worlds,
Into this wild abyss the wary fiend
Stood on the brink of Hell and looked a while,
Pondering his voyage; for no narrow frith

920 He had to cross. Nor was his ear less pealed
With noises loud and ruinous (to compare
Great things with small) than when Bellona storms,
With all her battering engines bent to rase
Some capital city; or less than if this frame
925 Of heaven were falling, and these elements
In mutiny had from her axle torn
The steadfast Earth. At last his sail-broad vans
He spreads for flight, and in the surging smoke
Uplifted spurns the ground, thence many a league
930 As in a cloudy chair ascending rides
Audacious, but that seat soon failing, meets
A vast vacuity: all unawares
Flutt'ring his pennons vain plumb down he drops
Ten thousand fathom deep, and to this hour
935 Down had been falling, had not by ill chance
The strong rebuff of some tumultuous cloud
Instinct with fire and nitre hurried him
As many miles aloft: that fury stayed,
Quenched in a boggy Syrtis, neither sea,
940 Nor good dry land: nigh foundered on he fares,
Treading the crude consistence, half on foot,
Half flying; behoves him now both oar and sail.
As when a gryphon through the wilderness
With wingèd course o'er hill or moory dale,
945 Pursues the Arimaspian, who by stealth
Had from his wakeful custody purloined
The guarded gold: so eagerly the fiend
O'er bog or steep, through strait, rough, dense, or rare,
With head, hands, wings, or feet pursues his way,
950 And swims or sinks, or wades, or creeps, or flies.

At length a universal hubbub wild
Of stunning sounds and voices all confused
Borne through the hollow dark assaults his ear

With loudest vehemence: thither he plies,
955   Undaunted to meet there whatever power
Or spirit of the nethermost abyss
Might in that noise reside, of whom to ask
Which way the nearest coast of darkness lies
Bordering on light; when straight behold the throne
960   Of Chaos, and his dark pavilion spread
Wide on the wasteful deep; with him enthroned
Sat sable-vested Night, eldest of things,
The consort of his reign; and by them stood
Orcus and Adès, and the dreaded name
965   Of Demogorgon; Rumour next and Chance,
And Tumult and Confusion all embroiled,
And Discord with a thousand various mouths.
T'whom Satan turning boldly, thus.

Satan: 'Ye powers
And spirits of this nethermost abyss,
970   Chaos and ancient Night, I come no spy,
With purpose to explore or to disturb
The secrets of your realm, but by constraint
Wandering this darksome desert, as my way
Lies through your spacious empire up to light,
975   Alone, and without guide, half lost, I seek
What readiest path leads where your gloomy bounds
Confine with Heaven; or if some other place
From your dominion won, th'ethereal King
Possesses lately, thither to arrive
980   I travel this profound, direct my course;
Directed no mean recompense it brings
To your behoof, if I that region lost,
All usurpation thence expelled, reduce
To her original darkness and your sway
985   (Which is my present journey) and once more
Erect the standard there of ancient Night.
Yours be th'advantage all, mine the revenge.'

Thus Satan; and him thus the anarch old
With faltering speech and visage incomposed
990   Answered.

Chaos: 'I know thee, stranger, who thou art,
That mighty leading angel, who of late
Made head against Heaven's King, though overthrown.
I saw and heard, for such a numerous host
Fled not in silence through the frighted deep
995   With ruin upon ruin, rout on rout,
Confusion worse confounded; and Heaven gates
Poured out by millions her victorious bands
Pursuing. I upon my frontiers here
Keep residence; if all I can will serve,
1000   That little which is left so to defend,
Encroached on still through our intestine broils
Weakening the sceptre of old Night: first Hell
Your dungeon stretching far and wide beneath;
Now lately heaven and earth, another world
1005   Hung o'er my realm, linked in a golden chain
To that side Heaven from whence your legions fell:
If that way be your walk, you have not far;
So much the nearer danger; go and speed;
Havoc and spoil and ruin are my gain.'

1010   He ceased; and Satan stayed not to reply,
But glad that now his sea should find a shore,
With fresh alacrity and force renewed
Springs upward like a pyramid of fire
Into the wild expanse, and through the shock
1015   Of fighting elements, on all sides round
Environed wins his way; harder beset
And more endangered, than when Argo passed
Through Bosphorus, betwixt the justling rocks:
Or when Ulýsses on the larboard shunned
1020   Charybdis, and by th'other whirlpool steered.

So he with difficulty and labour hard
Moved on, with difficulty and labour he;
But he once past, soon after when Man fell,
Strange alteration! Sin and Death amain
1025   Following his track, such was the will of Heaven,
Paved after him a broad and beaten way
Over the dark abyss, whose boiling gulf
Tamely endured a bridge of wondrous length
From hell continued reaching the utmost orb
1030   Of this frail world; by which the spirits perverse
With easy intercourse pass to and fro
To tempt or punish mortals, except whom
God and good angels guard by special grace.
But now at last the sacred influence
1035   Of light appears, and from the walls of Heaven
Shoots far into the bosom of dim night
A glimmering dawn; here nature first begins
Her farthest verge, and Chaos to retire
As from her outmost works a broken foe
1040   With tumult less and with less hostile din,
That Satan with less toil, and now with ease
Wafts on the calmer wave by dubious light
And like a weather-beaten vessel holds
Gladly the port, though shrouds and tackle torn;
1045   Or in the emptier waste, resembling air,
Weighs his spread wings, at leisure to behold
Far off th'empyreal Heaven, extended wide
In circuit, undetermined square or round,
With opal towers and battlements adorned
1050   Of living sapphire, once his native seat;
And fast by hanging in a golden chain
This pendent world, in bigness as a star
Of smallest magnitude close by the moon.
Thither full fraught with mischievous revenge,
1055   Accursed, and in a cursèd hour he hies.

Notes to Book I

Synopsis to Book I: the Argument

After he had published the first edition (which we are using here) Milton wrote an argument or synopsis of events to place at the beginning of each book in the second edition of 1674. As it is very stilted, I offer the following alternative:

After introducing the whole poem, which is to centre upon disobedience to God, Milton shows us Satan and his fellow rebel angels suffering the effects of their disobedience. They are lying on a lake of fire in Hell, having just been thrown out of Heaven by Christ for refusing to accept his authority and for trying to replace God the Father by their leader Lucifer, now called Satan. He is the first to recover and discusses their situation with Beëlzebub, his lieutenant. They fly to the shore from where Satan arouses his followers from the lake and musters them like an army. The leaders of the divisions are described, and they are all encouraged by Satan to continue the fight against God, and under the direction of Mammon they prepare a palace where they will debate what to do next.

Milton's Invocation: Lines 1–26

Milton starts his poem as Homer started the Classical Epic, the *Iliad* some 2000 years before (see Approaches p.167), by addressing ('invoking') a Muse, a Goddess personifying artistic inspiration. Milton distinguishes his as the true *Heavenly Muse* who had dictated the Bible (which he sees as a kind of sacred poetry) to Moses and its other 'authors'. Milton sees himself as a second Moses, inspired by this exalted Muse to make his poem far surpass Classical Epic in the grandeur of its theme. The first 16 lines are analysed in Approaches p.159.

> 2   **mortal**   deadly.
> 6   **heavenly Muse**   see headnote above.
> 4–5   **Eden**   the garden of Eden or Paradise, from where Adam and Eve were driven after they had eaten the fruit of the forbidden tree.

one greater Man   Christ, who restored us to the blissful seat of Heaven when he paid for this first sin by dying on the Cross (see Approaches p.150).

7   **Oreb ... Sinai**   places where *the shepherd* Moses is said to have seen God (*Exodus* 3, 19), so being inspired to write *Genesis*, which describes the beginning of the world. (For Bible text used in Notes, see Appendix p.195)

10-11   **Sion hill ... Siloa's brook**   places which inspired New Testament writers; Jesus (the *oracle of God*) taught at Sion (where the Temple stood) and cured a blind man close to (*fast by*) Siloa (*John* 9).

15   **th'Aonian mount**   Helicon, the mountain sacred to the Muses (see headnote).

18   The Holy Spirit living within the temple of the body.

19   **Instruct**   main verb which, like *sing* (6), *moved* (29), and *stirred* (35), is frequently placed at the beginning of the line.

21   **Dove-like**   in *Genesis* the creative *spirit of God moved upon the face of the waters*, and the dove showed Noah that the flood was over (*Genesis* 1:8).

21   **brooding**   meditating, but also sitting like a hen on her eggs; Milton may be alluding to the ancient idea that the world was born from an egg.

22-3   Perhaps a reference to Milton's own blindness, which also introduces his constant identification of God with light and upward movement (see Approaches p.146, p.152).

25-6   This is the purpose of the whole poem: to explain God's Providence, or care and plan for Mankind, which underlies the often painful *ways of God*.

The Scope of the Whole Poem: Lines 27–49

Milton now gives a brief synopsis of the story of the whole poem (see Synopsis pp.183-4). First, he tells us what is to come after the events of Books I and II: the corruption of Mankind in the garden of Eden by Satan, disguised as a *serpent* (see *Genesis* 3). Then he briefly explains Satan's motivation: *envy* of Mankind's happiness, and *revenge* against

God for having thrown him and his angel-supporters out of Heaven. They were punished in this way because he had led them in a rebellion against God which resulted in a war in Heaven (see Approaches p.148). Note the focus on *Man's first disobedience* (I 1); Satan is only introduced because Milton wants to explain how evil entered the world.

28	**Nor** not even.
29	**grandparents** Adam and Eve, from whom the whole human species was believed to be descended.
30-1	**fall off, transgress** desert, disobey.
32	**For one restraint ... besides?** because of a single restriction (on tasting one fruit); otherwise they had command of the Earth.
34-6	**Th'infernal serpent** Satan, who was the immediate *cause* (28) of Adam and Eve's eating the fruit (their *revolt*), disguised as a serpent. Note the qualities here ascribed to Satan (see Approaches pp.173-5).
33	**seduced** tempted to corruption.
36	**the mother of Mankind** Eve.
36	**what time** at the time when.
37	**host** army.
38-41	Satan had previously been an angel in Heaven who tried to become supreme over other angels (*his peers*), and, using his own *host* of rebel angels, believed (*trusted*) he could *oppose* and defeat *the most High* God himself (see Approaches p.148).
43	**Raised** stirred up (main verb).
44	**vain** unsuccessful.
44	**Him** Satan, object of *Hurled* (see Approaches p.158).
45	**th'ethereal** Heavenly (highest part of atmosphere).
46	**ruin** falling (see *Luke* 10:18: *I beheld Satan as lightning fall from Heaven*).
47-8	**perdition** loss.
48	**adamantine** fabulous unbreakable mineral (see *Jude*1:6 in Bible).

The First Description of Hell: Lines 50–83

As Milton says in the *Argument* (or synopsis)

> ... the poem hastes into the midst of things, presenting Satan with his angels now fallen into Hell, ... a place of utter darkness ... Here Satan with his angels lying on the burning lake, thunderstruck and astonished, after a certain space recovers.

Do you sympathize with Satan's position here? How pictorial do you find Milton's description of Hell? On Milton's strange and self-contradictory description, see Approaches pp.161-2.

50   **Nine times**   The rebel angels fell for nine days (VI 871) like the Titans, to whom they are frequently compared (see note to I 196-200); they are then chained for nine days on the burning lake, a punishment suggested by *Revelation* 20:10.

51   **horrid**   causing horror but also bristling, shaggy (because it is associated with hair standing up; one of Milton's favourite words).

53   **Confounded though immortal**   cast down although unable to die. The fallen angels are made of immortal fire (see Approaches pp.149-50), but since they sinned they can be cast down and in pain.

53-4   **doom/Reserved**   the judgement (*doom*) on him had preserved him to suffer more of God's wrath.

56-7   **his baleful eyes/That witnessed**   his eyes, both evil and in pain, expressed and saw the disaster.

59   **ken**   range of vision or knowledge.

64   **discover**   reveal.

65   **doleful**   sorrowful. Note the way the scenery suggests emotions (see Approaches p.162).

66-7   **hope never comes/That comes to all**   perhaps echoing the words inscribed above the gate of Dante's Hell: *All hope abandon ye who enter here*; see Approaches p.167.

68   **urges**   drives on (the sense of the Latin *urgeo*).

69   **sulphur**   brimstone, a corrosive chemical traditionally associated with Hell, which burns here without being used up (*unconsumed*).

71   **ordained**   ordered, prepared.

72   **portion**   place, fate.

73-4   The distance from Hell to Heaven is three times the distance from the centre of the Earth to the outermost orbit of the stars. See sketch on p.194. As in line 50, Milton's calculations are based on the mystical number 3.

75   **unlike**   the fallen angels will try to make it more like Heaven; see headnote to I 670-751, p.86.

78   **discerns**   makes out in the gloom.

78   **weltering**   wallowing helplessly.

81   **Beëlzebub**   'Lord of the Flies' and called 'Prince of the Demons' in *Mark* 3:22 (which is set in Palestine). He is Satan's second-in-command; see Approaches p.179.

81   **arch-enemy**   the supreme enemy. *Enemy* is the principal meaning of the name *Satan*, though Satan frequently tries to apply it to God (for example, I 122).

Satan's First Speech: Lines 84–126

These lines introduce us to two sides of Satan's character: is he the noble and suffering hero standing firm against overwhelming odds, or the deceitful politician disguising his failure from his closest friend? See Approaches p.175. He is already taking control of the angels' future, for he rejects some possible options (for example, 108, 111), and is only questioning whether to use *force* or *guile* in his continued war against God. This will be debated from II 41. The main points he makes are reinforced by Beëlzebub, and listed at headnote to I 127-55, p.62. Make a list of the ways he characterizes God (for example, *potent Victor in his rage* [95]); how far do these names help him to excuse his own failure?

84-94   **If thou beest he ...**   if you really are Beëlzebub, whom Satan says *misery hath joined* (main verb, 90) to him now, since God surprisingly proved stronger than them.

85-7   Satan used to be called Lucifer, 'light-bearer', and presumably Beëlzebub was nearly as bright in Heaven (the *happy realms of light*) if he shone brighter than the *myriads* (vast numbers) there.

87   **if he whom mutual league**   if you are really he who once *joined* (90) in alliance with me (but was it really *mutual*?) to

help each other in the *glorious enterprise* (88) to overthrow God.

92 **highth** height. Milton's spelling intensifies the highness.

93 **thunder** the *ten thousand thunders* of VI 836 with which Jesus cast out the rebel angels (described at 94 as *dire arms*).

94 **dire** terrible.

94-104 Fear will not cause Satan to *repent or change* (main verbs, 96) the mind that fought against God, because his pride (*disdain*) and *sense of injured merit* (98) persists. Satan was provoked to rebel by God's promotion of Jesus over himself (V 670), and claims that his fellow rebels would have preferred him to the tyrants, God and Jesus; see Approaches p.148.

95 **potent** powerful.

99-100 **contend, contention** oppose, opposition.

102 **durst** dared to.

104 **dubious** uncertain (but was it really uncertain?).

105 **field** battle.

109 'and what else cannot be overcome?'

111-16 Satan anticipates his soliloquy in Bk IV here (see Approaches pp.177-8) by saying it would indeed be ignoble to ask God for forgiveness on bended knee, since God (the *who* of 113) had so recently been afraid of him.

112 **deify** make divine (ironic, as God *is* divine).

115 **ignominy** disgrace.

116-21 **fate** (a power Satan prefers to God, see Approaches p.177) ensures that the angelic substance of *gods* (his name for the angels) cannot die, and as they will have improved in experience, so they may *with more successful hope* (120), continue the war with God, using either *force* or *guile*.

117 **empyreal substance** the pure fire out of which the highest heaven is made; see Approaches p.149.

118 **event** outcome.

119 **In arms ... advanced** our weapons are no worse and our understanding of the possible outcome is much better.

122 **Foe** see note to I 81.

124 **tyranny of Heaven** see Approaches p.140 for political implications.

126   **Vaunting**   boasting. This line sums up Satan's two sides; see Approaches pp.175–8 on Satan's despair.

Beëlzebub's First Speech: Lines 127–55

We discover here something of Beëlzebub's character and his relationship with Satan. See if you can find the following ideas expressed in both this speech and Satan's:

● a preference for seeing *Fate* or *Chance* as the supreme power
● the claim that God's victory was solely one of *strength*
● reliance on the immortality of their *heavenly essences*
● the belief that the mind can remain unchanged.

However, as Beëlzebub continues to speak, his view of the situation begins to differ from Satan's, particularly with regard to God's power. Can you see this happen? Once again it is worth listing the ways in which God is described.

128–42   Another very long and complex sentence; having addressed Satan for six lines, Beëlzebub reaches his main point at 134 (main verbs *see* and *rue*).

128   **throned powers**   rulers in the hierarchy of angels. Heaven is organized like an army (see Approaches p.148).

129   **th'embattled seraphim**   armed angels (the *seraphim* were the second highest rank.

130   **conduct**   leadership (Latin *duco* I lead).

132   **his**   God's.

134   **rue**   regret.

138   **heavenly essences**   another way of referring to the *empyreal substance* explained in note to I 117.

140   **vigour**   physical strength. Beëlzebub here takes pride in their returning strength, but begins at 146 to wonder why it is returning. For the answer see note to 210–13 below.

141   **glory extinct**   their brightness has been extinguished (see line 97).

144   **Of force**   perforce, by necessity.

143–7   Beëlzebub is afraid that their returning strength will enable them to endure or *support* increased torture, or even to perform God's *errands* (as perhaps they will; see note to I 210–13 and Approaches p.151). What does this tell you about his attitude to God?

146   **entire** undamaged.

148   **suffice his vengeful ire** satisfy his wrathful and sadistic passion for revenge.

149–50   **thralls/By right of war** contemporary prisoners of war could, in theory, be made the slaves (*thralls*) of the conquerors.

153   **avail** benefit.

Satan's Returning Decision and Freedom: Lines 156–91

Satan's reply begins to explain why and how he will continue his opposition to God. Lines 162–8 should be read in conjunction with 211–20, which states God's counter-policy (see Approaches p.151). What does Satan's policy suggest to you? Is it childish? spiteful? heroic in the face of overwhelming odds? What does it tell you about Satan's feeling for God?

157   **Fallen cherub** Beëlzebub, whom Satan is addressing.

157–8   **weak is miserable/Doing or suffering** This is one of a number of places where a contrast can be drawn between Satan and Christ, who did not despise weakness. Doing/suffering (or active/passive) represents the contrasting types of human behaviour; you can use this opposition to analyse the debate between the angels in Book II: some want to *do* and some to *suffer* (see II 199).

159   **aught** anything.

162–8   God's caring plan for creation (his *Providence*), explained by Milton I 211–20 will indeed seek *out of our evil … to bring forth good*. Satan plans to *pervert that end* by frustrating God wherever possible in order to *grieve him* and *disturb* his plans (*inmost counsels*).

169–70   **angry Victor** God, as Satan presents him, for God is in fact mercifully calling back the angelic pursuers, who are therefore not acting as agents (*ministers*) of vengeance at all.

171-3   **sulphurous hail ... o'erblown hath laid/The fiery surge**
the sulphur-rain that was *shot after us* has blown itself out, so
that the lake of fire (*fiery surge*) is now calm (*laid*). The
weather is improving.

175-6   This suggests a cartoon picture, in which the thunderbolts
have lightning wings. Satan hopes it has run out of missiles
(*spent his shafts*), thus concealing again the fact that God
must be easing their torments on purpose.

176   **his**   its (a relatively new word which Milton avoids).

177   **bellow ... boundless deep**   to resonate through Hell (the
open vowels echo the meaning).

178   **slip**   miss. What does this tell you of Satan's character?

178-9   **scorn,/Or satiate fury**   Satan calls God's mercy *scorn* and
suggests that his sadistic appetite is simply satisfied (*satiate*)
for the moment.

180   **dreary plain**   Satan chooses this plain, which is described
in emotional as well as physical terms, as the assembly
ground for his troops.

181   **seat**   place.

181   **void**   empty.

182   **save**   except.

182   **livid**   bluish leaden colour.

183   **Thither ... tend**   Let us go there.

185   **rest**   Hell is characterized by change and restlessness; see
Approaches pp.146-7, pp.179-80.

187-91   **Consult**   main verb at beginning of line. But is Satan really
going to consult his fellow angels? What decisions must he
already have made to be now consulting on the issues which
are outlined here?

189   **dire**   terrible.

190   **reinforcement**   encouragement.

191   **despair**   emphasized by rhyme with *repair* (188). Why is
this passion so appropriate to Satan and to Hell, and how is
it related to *hope* (189)? (See Approaches pp.175-80.)

First Description of Satan: Lines 192–241

This passage includes the first **epic similes**, elaborate comparisons usually introduced by *As* and completed by *So*; see Approaches pp.169–70. By looking at all the features which Satan has in common with the Titans, with Leviathan, or with a volcano, you can uncover what Milton is telling us about Satan apart from the fact that he is very big.

Milton also confronts here the central problem of why God allowed Satan to exist at all, let alone to have his freedom (*Left him at large*, 213). The principal answer given here is that this policy would ultimately allow God to show a much greater *grace* when he redeems the world by the sacrifice of Christ, but see Approaches pp.150–2 for a wider discussion.

193–5   **up-lift ... Prone**   head lifted up, body lying flat. What does this position suggest to you? Compare it with the next images of Satan rearing up and then flying to land (221, 225).

196   **rood**   rod, an ancient unit of measurement, equal to about five metres.

197–200   **As**   introduces the first epic simile, comparing Satan to *Titanian ... Briarios or Typhon*, two giant-monsters of the Titan race; Briareos had 100 arms, Typhon (who lived at *Tarsus*) 100 heads. The Titans deposed their father-king (Uranus), and later their new king (Saturn) was himself deposed by his son, Zeus. See I 508–14 and Approaches pp.169–70.

200–8   **Leviathan**   enormous Biblical sea-monster generally identified with the whale, and to which Milton attaches the Scandinavian (and *Arabian Nights*) fairy tale of a monster as big as an island, which deceives sailors into mooring to its hide (*rind*) before swimming away with them. The sentence-structure goes: *the pilot* (subject) *Moors* (main verb at beginning of line) by *Him* (= Leviathan) while he is *slumbering* (203).

203   **haply**   by chance.

204   **night-foundered skiff**   a small boat disabled and leaking at night. Satan is often associated with night and the sea.

205   **Deeming**   believing.

207   **under the lea**   on the side sheltered from the wind.

208   **Invests**   clothes.

209   **So**   marks the end of these epic similes.

210-13   **nor ever thence/Had risen**   nor would ever have risen from there. Milton here intrudes his own voice to answer Beëlzebub's question at 143-52 and Satan's boast at 162-68; Milton follows St. Augustine in the belief that ultimately everything which happens is within God's plan or *Providence* (see Approaches pp.151-2).

213   **at large**   at liberty.

214   **reiterated**   repeated.

216   **enraged**   filled with rage.

219   **On Man by him seduced**   God's *grace* will be shown to man because he was induced to commit sin (*seduced*) by Satan.

221   **Forthwith**   straight away.

221   **rears**   raises, lifts (his *mighty stature*).

222-4   Satan's sudden movement creates a trough bristling with fire (*horrid vale*) and surrounded by flames sloping away from it.

226   **incumbent**   leaning on the air.

228   **He lights**   he alights, touches down, on the burning 'land' which surrounds the lake of fire.

230-7   This third epic simile appears to elaborate on Satan's *hue* (colour, 230) but is really a comparison of his movement with that of the torn mountainsides which Milton imagines would fly through the air when the Sicilian volcanoes *Pelorus* and *Etna* erupt. Milton had visited Sicily, but look for the words which suggest not eruption so much as an industrial explosion, or the belching and farting demons of Hieronymous Bosch (see picture on p.193 and Approaches pp.162-3).

231   **subterranean wind**   underground force (but why *wind*?).

233-4   **combustible ... Sublimed**   The inflammable fuel in the centre of the mountain is ignited by the underground *wind* and immediately becomes flame and vapour.

236-7   **singed bottom all involved**   the burnt floor, wrapped in *stench and smoke* (again note the body-language) where the mountainside had been.

237 **such resting** ironic, as there is no rest in Hell (see I 66).

239 **glorying to have scaped** triumphant in their escape, as at I 240-1.

239 **Stygian flood** Hellish lake (alluding to the Greek Underworld river, the Styx).

241 **sufferance of supernal Power** the permission of almighty Power (referring to line 213 above).

Satan Takes Possession of his New Kingdom: Lines 242-82

Here, as so often, Satan seems to see the truth only to manipulate it. How does he convey his sense of a real loss, but immediately excuse or justify himself, or in other ways change the facts? How far do you agree with Satan's assertion that *Here at least/We shall be free* (258-9)? This is also one of several passages which 'internalize Hell' by suggesting it is essentially within the mind (see Approaches p.162). The speech is discussed as a whole in Approaches p.140. This exchange with Beëlzebub displays not only Satan's concern for his *associates and co-partners* (265), but also (according to the flattering Beëlzebub) his power over them. Do you think he is misusing it here?

242 **clime** climate.

244-5 **gloom ... light** it shows that Satan is still partly good that he recognizes the essential superiority of light over darkness; Mammon confuses the distinction II 262-8.

246-7 **dispose and bid/What shall be right** Satan asserts that God wilfully arranges and decides what is right (rather than acting righteously because he is good).

248 Satan claims equality with God in all but strength; compare I 92, 133, 258.

253 **A mind not to be changed** This is both heroic and deeply ironic; changelessness is an attribute of Heaven only, and Satan changes and deteriorates before our eyes; compare this

speech with the spitefulness and lies of his thoughts in Bk II (see Approaches pp.146-7).

254-5   The truth that *the mind is its own place* explains how Satan could invent Sin in Heaven, and later suggests true hope for Adam, who *is* told he *shalt possess/A Paradise within thee happier far* than the one he lost (XII 586-7).

258   **thunder**   see note to I 93.

259   **free** suggests the ideals of the Commonwealth; see Approaches p.139.

261   **we may reign secure**   how do you see the plural *we* here?

262   **worth ambition**   worth being ambitious for.

263   **Better to reign in Hell**   This sounds Classically heroic; Caesar supposedly said 'I would rather be first in this miserable village than second in Rome' (Plutarch *Life* XI 2, or see Homer's *Odyssey* XI 489-91). But in a religious context it suggests a 'service to sin' (*Romans* 6) rather than the 'perfect freedom' of service to God (*Book of Common Prayer*). Mammon later describes what he thinks it would be like to *serve in Heaven*; see II 237-43 and Approaches pp.142-3.

266   **astonished**   stunned

266   **th'oblivious pool**   they lie forgetful on the lake of fire (a **transferred epithet**; see Approaches p.161 for a definition).

267-9   **call them not ... to try**   follows *wherefore* of 264: 'why do we not call them to try once more?'

268   **mansion**   dwelling (where they *manent*, from *manere* (Latin) meaning to remain).

269   **rallied arms**   reassembled weapons.

273   **Which but ... foiled**   which none but the All-powerful could have prevented from winning.

274   **liveliest pledge**   most vital promise. Beëlzebub claims that Satan's voice alone rallies the angels in tight corners (*worst extremes, perilous edge/Of battle, all assaults*, 276-7).

278   **resume**   main verb, following *If* (274): 'they will become brave again.'

280   **yon**   yonder.

281   **erewhile**   previously.

282   **pernicious highth**   deadly height.

Second Description of Satan and His Awakening of the Fallen Angels: Lines 283–330

This passage, with its Classical and Biblical epic similes (see Approaches p.169) and its wonderful speech (see Approaches p.147), is one of the most heroic in the poem. Yet there may be other elements in the description of Satan and the angels, or in his address to them, which give you a more negative impression. Are the angels the victims of Satan's egotism, or are they being helped by him to recover their self-esteem and ability to act? The passage also introduces the story of the Flight from Egypt by Moses and the Jewish people, which is the source of many comparisons in I and II (see Approaches pp.169–70 for an outline).

283   **superior fiend**   Satan now walks to the *shore* of the burning lake, from where he had flown to the *dreary plain* (180).

284–6   **ponderous shield ... Behind him cast**   he carried his weighty shield, hardened in heavenly fire (*Ethereal temper*), over his shoulder. Achilles, the hero of Homer's *Iliad*, has a similarly mighty shield which is described at length.

287–91   Epic simile introduced by *like* comparing the shield to the moon. Milton visited the then blind *Tuscan artist*, or astronomer, Galileo, in Florence (situated in Valdarno in Tuscany) in 1638, and was probably allowed to view the moon through the telescope (*optic glass*), which Galileo was believed to have invented, from the nearby hill at *Fésolé* (Fiesole). This passage and Satan's associations with night and the moon are discussed in Approaches pp.169–70.

292–5   Compared to his spear, the tallest pine cut (*hewn*) in Norway to be a mast for an *ammiral* (flagship) would have looked like a small stick (*wand* – no magical connotations). The size-shifting in these two similes is significant. The moon is bigger than the shield; the tree is smaller than the spear. It is as if Milton is using the telescope at both ends to create a dream-like effect.

296   **marl**   earth.

297   **azure**   blue.

297–8   **torrid clime ... vaulted with fire**   Satan is painfully affected by the scorchingly hot climate under the fiery roof of Hell.

299   **Nathless**   nevertheless.

302   **autumnal leaves**   The first of three epic similes for the fallen angels. They lie stunned (*entranced*), as *thick* as the golden leaves on the valley floor at *Vallombrosa* (or 'valley of shadows') in Etruria or Tuscany. Vergil also compares the dead to fallen leaves; see Appendix pp.196–7 and ask yourself whether the effect is the same in both. For Milton's enjoyment of names, see Approaches p.156.

304   **scattered sedge**   the angels are thrown about like waterweed after a storm (associated with the appearance of the star-constellation *Orion*, who is *armed* with a sword).

307   **Busiris and his Memphian chivalry**   Pharaoh and the Egyptian troops (who drowned when Moses closed the waters of the Red Sea on them; *Exodus* 14).

308   **perfidious hatred**   treacherous hostility; the Egyptians, like Satan's army, broke their word to God (to let the Jews leave).

309   **sojourners of Goshen**   the Jews, who journeyed to Goshen on the far side of the Nile.

313   **amazement**   shock, bewilderment; also suggests wandering in a maze.

315–6   **Princes, potentates**   As usual, Satan begins his speech with a flattering **exordium** or address; see outline of speech-construction at the beginning of the Notes for Book II. What emotions does Satan appeal to in this speech?

319–20   **to repose/Your wearied virtue**   one of several sarcastic taunts (continuing until 325); do you think it would be better or worse if Satan apologized for the defeat?

322–3   **abject, adore**   the assonance on *a* links the two words, suggesting one has to be thrown down (*abject*) to worship. See Approaches p.156 on assonance.

324   **Cherub and seraph**   angelic beings.

325   **anon**   soon. Satan is alerting them to immediate danger.

325   **arms and ensigns**   weapons and flags.

326–7   **discern/Th'advantage**   see that we are at their mercy.

328   **linked thunderbolts**   By taking the 'bolts' literally, Milton suggests chains made of thunder.

330   **Awake, arise**   note the arousing rhythm of this line.

The Fallen Angels Rally and Assemble before Satan: Lines 331–75

The angels seem to feel guilty (*abashed, found by whom they dread*); is this appropriate? The epic similes (see Approaches pp.169-71) which describe them concentrate on their immense numbers, and yet comparisons with *locusts* and barbarian hordes from the *frozen loins* of the North, diminish our respect for them (numberlessness is discussed in Approaches p149). Milton then introduces the next substantial section of the poem, by explaining he will call the fallen angels by the *new names* of the pagan gods which they supposedly later became according to one tradition; can Milton possibly believe this to be literally true?

335-6   There are two double negatives here which cancel each other out (see Approaches p.159), so that the angels do *perceive their plight* and *feel* their *pains*.

338-44   An epic simile comparing the fallen angels to the plague of locusts which Moses (*Amram's son*) called up by his supernaturally-powerful (*potent*) rod to help persuade the *impious Pharaoh* to let the Jews go (*Exodus* 6:20, 10:12-15 and see Approaches p.171). Can you think of other points of comparison, besides their being *numberless*, between the fallen angels and a mass of insects which darken the sky, and then eat all the crops?

340   **pitchy**   black.

341   **warping**   whirling through the air like snow.

342   **impious**   irreligious (both because Pharaoh is a pagan, and because he breaks his oath to the Jews and their God).

345   **cope**   canopy.

346   **nether**   lower.

348   **sultan**   despot.

349   **in even balance down they light**   they alight in an ordered formation (at a signal from Satan's spear).

351-5   An epic simile comparing the angels to the *multitude* of barbarian invaders whom Machiavelli had described coming from the lands north of the Rhine and Danube (*Rhene or the Danaw*) to overturn the Roman Empire as far south as North Africa (*the Libyan sands*).

352   **frozen loins**   cold womb; perhaps rather extreme language for North Germany, but it is the first of a series of images suggesting 'false creativity' or sterility; see Approaches pp.162-3.

357   **the heads and leaders thither haste**   The leaders of each division of Satan's army advance quickly to be reviewed.

359   **princely dignities**   of royal status.

360   **erst**   before.

361-3   **their names ... and rased ... from the Books of Life.**   The names they had in Heaven, such as Lucifer (which was Satan's), have been deleted from God's book of the blessed (see *Revelation* 21:27 and Approaches p.148).

364   **sons of Eve**   derogatory term for Mankind (because Eve was faithless).

365   **new names**   see headnote.

366   **God's high sufferance for the trial of Man**   God's allowance of liberty to the fallen angels so they can test Mankind; see I 213 and Approaches p.138, p.151.

369-70   **th'invisible ... to transform**   The fallen angels, by telling lies (*falsities*, 367) persuade men to worship them in the form of idols decorated with tinsel (*gay religions*, 372), instead of the invisible true God. Milton, as a Protestant, may be thinking of the Catholics as well as pagans here; see Approaches pp.143-4).

The Parade of Angels as Pagan Gods: Lines 376–521

A new invocation *Say Muse* (see note to I 6) alerts us to a new episode, a catalogue of heroes typical of Classical epic (see Approaches p.171). As explained in the previous headnote, Milton is using an old tradition that *long after* the fall of the angels from Heaven, they were worshipped on Earth as the pagan gods. Satan's commanders are a select group of these: the pagan gods chosen for worship by the Jewish kings themselves, who had temples near or even on Mount Sion, where the Temple to Jehovah stood (*I Kings* 11:7–9; *II Kings* 18: 10–18;. 21:1–5). The implication is that if even God's chosen people, the Jews, chose to follow pagan gods and the vices they represent, then Christians nowadays might also be tempted to follow the 'gods' of violence, self-indulgence, materialism, and so forth. Satan's commanders are, therefore, the representatives not of heroic but of degraded human qualities (see Approaches p.178). As you read keep thinking of the modern equivalents.

The whole passage (like its parallel in *Nativity Ode* 197–228) exhibits Milton's knowledge of Hebrew and Jewish scholarship, but maybe the place-names are chosen as much for their music as their authenticity (see Approaches p.156). As it is is very long, I have divided it into sub-sections [a)–f)] after a brief introductory section.

377   **fiery couch**   the burning lake.
379   **Came singly**   each named leader comes before Satan in the parade in order of importance (*worth*, 378).
379   **strand**   beach.
380   **promiscuous**   undiscriminated.
382   **prey**   human beings to tempt and corrupt.
385   **durst abide**   dared endure (by being so close).
386–7   **throned/Between the cherubim**   There were gold cherubim at each end of the sacred Ark of the Covenant in the Temple which was on Mount *Sion* (*Psalm* 80:1) .
388–9   **Within his sanctuary**   Altars to pagan gods were actually set up within the Temple itself (see *II Kings* 21:1–5).
389   **Abominations**   pagan gods (the word used in the Authorized Version quoted in the next headnote).
391   **affront**   insult.

a) Moloch and Chemos: Lines 392–418

Milton puts at the front the gods whose temples were the greatest *affront* (391) to *Jehovah*, the true God. In *Kings* 11:7–9 Solomon (under his wives' influence, of course) built *a high place for Chemos, the abomination of Moab, in the hill that is before Jerusalem, and for Moloch, the abomination of the children of Ammon. And likewise did he for all his foreign wives, who burned incense and sacrificed unto their gods. And the Lord was angry with Solomon.* What vices do these two gods suggest to you?

392-4   **Moloch** See Approaches pp.178-9. Milton follows the historian Sandys in describing him as an idol with a furnace in his chest in which children were burned as sacrifices while priests drowned their cries *with the continual clang of trumpets and timbrels* (tambourines). (See *A Relation of a Journey* (1637), Fowler edition of *P.L.*)

392   **horrid king** horrific king (*Moloch* means *king*).

396   **Ammonite** followers of Moloch living in *Rabba*, the *city of waters* (*II Samuel* 12:27) and in Argob and Basan, which were also in Judah (*Judges* 11:13).

400   **Audacious neighbourhood** presumptuous position (in Judah).

403   **opprobrious hill** (*hill of scandal* at 416) the shameful idol-covered *hill before Jerusalem* (see headnote a), later the Mount of Olives, *against* (opposite) Jehovah's Temple on Mount Sion .

404-5   The valley that divided these hills was therefore discredited, lost the name *Hinnon*, and acquired the shameful names *Tophet* and *Gehenna* which were associated with Hell.

406   **Chemos** the Moabite god; see headnote a) and *Numbers* 21:29.

407-11   These Biblical place-names, like *Sittim* (413) were associated with the Moabites.

411   **th'asphaltic pool** the Dead Sea, which contains bitumens (inflammable) minerals, such as asphalt.

412   **Peor** Baal-Peor was another name for Chemos, whom the Jews briefly worshipped during their escape from Egypt.

414-15   **wanton rites, lustful orgies** sexual licence associated with Chemos/Peor.

414   **cost them woe** The Jews who worshipped Peor were punished by a plague (*woe*); see *Numbers* 25:1-9.

416   **hill of sandal** see note to I 403.

417   **lust hard by hate** The two temples, to Moloch and to

Chemos, like these vices they represent, were very close (*hard by*) to each other.

418 **Josiah** the king who destroyed the two temples and turned the valley to a rubbish dump (*II Kings* 23:13).

b) Baalim, Ashtaroth, and Thammuz: Lines 419–56

Milton now considers the sun-gods *Baalim* (plural of the generalized name Baal, 'Lord'), and the moon-goddess *Ashtareth* (plural *Ashtoreth*) who loved the beautiful youth *Thammuz*. They were worshipped in the area stretching from Canaan up as far as the Euphrates, and the cult of Thammuz in particular was associated with excessive emotionalism. Is Milton raising the question of which vices are 'gender-specific'? But if so, why is he so insistent that neither evil nor good spirits have any particular name, number, gender or shape (421–31)? Where in Books I and II do we see the angels change shape or size, becoming *dilated* or *condensed*? (See Approaches pp.149–50 for discussion.)

420 **brook** the river Besor (*I Samuel* 30:10).

423 **spirits** good as well as bad angels.

425 **essence** the *quintessence* (III 716) or *empyreal substance* (I 117) from which the angels are made. As Raphael explains in more detail in VIII 620–9 it is so pure (*uncompounded*) that angels can flow into one another when making love (see Approaches p.150).

426 **manacled** As Man, unlike the angels, is a mixture of soul and body, his hands (*mains*) and other limbs act as handcuffs (*manacles*) chaining the free spirit inside the body.

427 **founded on ... the brittle strength** based on fragile physical strength (as opposed to the *living strength* of God (433; see *I Samuel* 15:29).

431 **love or enmity** depending on whether they are good or evil spirits.

432–7 **For those** for Baal and Ashtareth (see *Judges* 2:13–14 where the Jews *forsook the Lord, and served Baal and Ashtareth ... And the Lord delivered them into the hands of spoilers ... and enemies.*

435 **bestial** beast-like in form or nature (as *bestial* at I 481).

438–9 **Astoreth ... Astartè** The moon, here a horned goddess, is often associated with women (who have a monthly cycle).

Phoenecia is on the coast of Syria and contains the city of Sidon (hence *Sidonian*).

442–3 **Sion ... offensive mountain** see note to 403 above.

444 **uxorious** over-fond of his (700) wives (see headnote a).

446 **Thammuz** The youth known in Greece as *Adonis*, whom *Astarte* loved and revived from death; this was celebrated annually as part of a fertility cult in Lebanon in late summer, when the Adonis river runs red with earth, suggesting his blood running from the boar-wound which had killed him (*yearly wounded*, 452).

453 **Infected Sion's daughters** The Jewish women (*Sion's daughters*) also began to express sorrow (*like heat*) for Thammuz, and this led to sexual rites which Ezekiel saw in a vision (*Ezekiel* 8:14). What is the connection which Milton seems to be making between sorrow and sex here?

457 **alienated Judah** the Jews in exile in Babylon.

c) Dagon and Rimmon: Lines 457–76

The Philistines of Palestine (which contained the cities *Azotus, Gath, Ascalon, Accaron,* and *Gaza*) captured the holy Ark of the Jews, their traditional enemies, and put it in the temple of Dagon. The next morning the idol had lost its human head and hands; only its fish-tail was left (*I Samuel* 5:1–5). Rimmon was a Damascan god whom the Jewish king Ahaz worshipped (so that he *gained a king*).

459 **Maimed** see headnote c).

460 **grunsel** threshold.

467 **Him followed** came after Dagon (who presumably jumps along on his tail).

467–71 Rimmon's temple (*delightful seat*) was in Damascus on the confluence of the rivers *Abbana* and *Pharphar*, in which the leper Naaman said he would prefer to bathe, after Elisha told him to bathe in the Jordan – which he eventually did and was cured (*II Kings* 5:1–19) and so *lost* to Rimmon's worship.

472 **Ahaz his sottish conqueror** The foolish Ahaz who displaced one of Jehovah's altars in the Temple by a copy of Rimmon's altar, although he had *vanquished* (476) Damascas

and so should have appreciated the superiority of Jehovah
(see *II Kings* 16:10–15).

d) The Egyptian Gods: Lines 476–89

Milton identifies the Golden Calf worshipped by the Jews in *Oreb*
(*Exodus* 32:1–6) with the *brutish* bovine gods of Egypt, from where they
were escaping. Thus, like the gods he has mentioned, these too repre-
sent a false choice made by the 'people of God' in the Bible. Since Man
is distinguished from beasts by his soul and his reason, to choose to
worship a beast is to deliberately degenerate. What modern equivalent
can you think of for such a false choice?

478	**Osiris, Isis, Orus** *Osiris* was worshipped as a bull, *Isis* had cow's horns, and *Orus* was their calf-child.
479–80	**abused/Fanatic Egypt** deceived the extremist priests of Egypt. The fallen angels took animal shapes (*monstrous ... brutish*) or heads, and induced the Egyptians to worship them.
481	**wandering gods** Isis wandered the world seeking the parts of Osiris' body.
481	**brutish forms** see headnote d) and note to I 435.
483	**Th'infection** see note to 453 above.
483	**borrowed** the priest Aaron took the golden earrings of the Jews to make the golden calf; see headnote d).
484	**rebel king** Jeroboam, who later set up two (*doubled*) golden calves, in *Bethel* and *Dan* in Sumaria (*I Kings* 12:20–29). These, like the original Golden Calf, were said to have deliv-ered the Jews from Egypt (*Psalm* 106:20).
487–9	On the 'Passover' night God *passed* over the Jewish houses, but made the Egyptian first-born as dead (*equalled*) as their own gods; this *stroke* was the real reason for the Jews' deliver-ance from Egypt (*Exodus* 12:29–33).
489	**bleating** cry of calves as well as sheep.

e) Belial: Lines 490–505

Belial has no altar because he was not really a distinct god in the Bible;
the phrase *the sons/Of Belial* (501–2) seems to represent people
enslaved to a group of vices rather than a specific idol. Using the
Biblical references Milton invents a new character, and gives him the

vices of the rich *in courts and palaces*: atheism, gluttony, luxury, lust, violence, drunkenness, and sodomy. Are these the vices he displays in Book II (see II 198-218 and Approaches pp.178-9). What does the phrase *to love/ Vice for itself* (491-2) suggest to you?

490   **last**   of the named gods/angels.

491   **gross**   blatant.

495   **Eli's sons**   sons of the priest who preferred to eat rather than to sacrifice holy animals (*I Samuel* 2:12-17), suggesting the vice of greed.

500   **injury and outrage**   insults and violation of others' rights.

500   **night**   as usual (for example, I 440 above) Milton associates vice with darkness; see Approaches p.169.

502   **flown**   'high flown' or 'high' in the modern sense.

503-5   **Sodom, Gibeah**   In both cities a woman is offered to the *sons of Belial* by a *hospitable* Jew wishing to protect male guests from homosexual (*worse*) rape (*Genesis* 19:4-11; *Judges* 19: 22-28).

f) The Classical Gods: Lines 506-21

Having named the Biblical gods, Milton describes the Classical gods much more briefly, because the Jews never followed them. Why also might he not not want to associate them with vice or betrayal?

508   **Ionian Gods**   the Olympian Gods.

508   **Javan**   a descendant of Noah and the supposed ancestor of the Greek race (*Genesis* 10:2).

508   **held**   believed.

509-10   **Gods ... first born**   they admitted themselves that they were younger than Uranus (*Heaven*) and Ge (*Earth*), whom they proudly claimed as their great-grandparents (their parents were the Titans).

510-14   **Saturn**   the youngest of the Titans, said here to be the children (*brood*) of Uranus' eldest son, *Titan*. Saturn deposed his father and was himself deposed in the same way (*like measure*) by Zeus, the son he had by *Rhea*. These *usurping* acts repeat the sin of Satan; see note to I 196-200 and Approaches p.169.

514-15   **Crete/And Ida**   Mount Ida in Crete was believed to be the birthplace of Zeus (and tourists are even shown his bath).

516 **Olympus** The gods supposedly inhabited the highest mountain in Greece, Olympus, which is always snow-covered.

516-17 **middle air ... heaven** the air at the level of mountain tops which is the part inhabited by spirits who cannot reach the *empyrean* (God's Heaven).

517-19 **Delphi, Dodona** places in Greece (*Doric land*) where the Classical gods were *renowned* (507) for oracles. Note the dreamy effect of the alliteration.

519 **or who** further examples of *The rest* (507), this time from outside Greece.

519-21 After being deposed, Saturn fled over the Adriatic Sea (*Adria*) to Italy (*th'Hesperian fields*) and France (*Celtic*) to Britain (*utmost isles*) where he may still lie asleep on Anglesey.

Satan Comforts and Marshals the Fallen Angels: Lines 522-87

Satan seems here to show genuine concern for his army, and he encourages them by calling them to arms, though as usual there are words which might undermine this positive impression. Should we be impressed by him? Should we feel an increasing admiration for the angels? They do seem to be trying to recover from their *abject posture* on the burning lake, when their arms lay *scattered* around them (see I 322, 325). There are a number of upward-moving (for example *upreared*, *upsent*) and brightening (*meteor*, *lustre*) words associated with them, but perhaps this recovery should be seen as superficial and temporary. Why does Milton compare them to armies which seem more fictional than real – first the Classical soldiers dancing to *Doric* music, and then the armies of Italian epics and English and French Romances (see Approaches p.167)? Should we be thinking of the heroic qualities and vast spectacle of such armies, or of their unreality?

523 **such wherein** such *looks* (522) in which.

525 **despair** See note to I 126.

527 **like doubtful hue** the same ambiguous expression.

527-8 **wonted pride/Soon recollecting** quickly summoning up his usual pride.

529 **Semblance ... not substance** the appearance of value, not the reality.

528-30 What do *gently* and *dispelled* tell you about Satan? Why does Milton feel he must interpose his own voice to discredit Satan's words as having *Semblance of worth, not substance* (they only seemed valuable and true)?

531 **straight** immediately.

532 **clarions** shrill military trumpets.

533-6 **standard ... imperial ensign** Satan's personal flag.

534 **Azazel** one of Satan's four standard bearers according to Jewish 'cabbalistic' (occult) writings, in which Milton was keenly interested.

537-9 The flag was decorated (*emblazed*) like a Roman standard with jewels, shining gold thread, coats of arms, and battle souvenirs. What does the comparison to a meteor suggest to you (see note to I 594-9 for one suggestion)?

540 **Sonorous metal** the resonant instruments mentioned in 532 above.

541 **the universal host upsent** the whole army sent up (the last word is turned round to fit the metre; see Approaches p.155.

542 **tore Hell's concave** penetrated the arched roof (see I 298).

543 **reign of Chaos** the kingdom outside Hell, ruled by Chaos and his consort, Night (we visit them II 959-63; see Approaches p.180).

546 **orient** lustrous, bright.

547 **helms** helmets.

548 **serried** close-packed.

549 **depth immeasurable** impossible to measure the width of the column. One of several places where Milton suggests that the fallen angels are numberless; see Approaches p.149).

550 **In perfect phalanx ... mood** in exact formation to appropriate modal music. The Dorian mode (*mood*), which is the white-note scale beginning on D, was associated in ancient

Greece with military music.

551-9   Milton, an ardent musician (see Approaches p.153), here describes the effect of music, as he does again II 546-54; in both cases emotions are controlled and soothed (*swage*) rather than aroused. The Dorian music here also seems able to control virtue, by transforming the emotion of rage into a steely composure (*noblest temper*) and willed courage (*deliberate valour*). Aristotle said that this mode induced a *settled temper* and Plato said it gave courage. (Prince ed. of *P.L.*)

556-7   **Not wanting ... thoughts**   not lacking power to lessen and soothe *troubled thoughts* by brief serious phrases (*touches*).

558   Note the soothing effect of the repeated *and*.

560-1   **Breathing united force ... in silence**   Compare Homer's *Iliad* 3:8: *The Greeks marched in silence, breathing courage*.

561   **charmed**   Are the angels being deluded by the music?

563   **horrid front**   the front line bristling with spears (see note to I 51).

568   **traverse**   across.

570   **visages and stature**   faces and size.

571   **number**   See note to 549 above.

572-3   **Distends ... and hardening**   enlarges, puffs up, and then hardens (compare *Daniel* 5:20 where God deposes King Nebbuchadnezzar because *his heart was lifted up, and his mind hardened in pride*). But do you altogether despise Satan here?

573-6   **for never ... cranes**   For never since the creation of Man could a concentrated (*embodied*) human force be assembled which, when compared to these, would be worth more than the Pigmy army. Pigmies are a race of very small people in Africa; who (according to *Iliad* III 1-5) were frequently attacked and defeated by flocks of cranes (birds); they are referred to again I 780.

575   **infantry**   foot-soldiers (with a pun on infant, suggesting smallness).

576   **though**   even if; introduces a comparison of Satan's army with the lesser ones of the Greek, Arthurian, and French legends.

576-8   **Giant brood ... Ilium**   even if the Titans (already mentioned 198 and 511) who fought the Olympian gods at Phlegra were joined with the gods and Greek heroes who fought at Thebes and Troy (*Ilium*).

579 **auxiliar** helping (according to Homer, the Greek gods were involved in these human wars).

579 **resounds** is famous.

579-81 **romance of Uther's son** stories (known collectively as *romances*) of King Arthur, son of Uther Pendragon, and his surrounding (*begirt*) Round Table of knights from Britain and Brittany (*Armorica*).

581 **begirt** surrounded.

583 **Jousted** fought on horseback with lances.

582-7 Milton finally refers to the legendary armies of the ninth-century Emperor Charlemagne (*Charlemain*), who defended France from Muslim (*infidel*) and African invaders till he and his 12 chief knights (*peerage*) were defeated at Roncesvalles (not *Fontarabbia*). The hypnotic place-names are mostly from Italian epics like *Orlando Furioso* (see Approaches p.167).

585 **Biserta** the port from which the African king Agramante embarked.

Third Description of Satan: He Weeps for his Army: Lines 587–621

Here we are told of the physical and moral degeneration of Satan, but we may feel how much remains (including what remains of his virtue) rather than how much is lost. The comparisons of Satan with a tower and the obscured sun suggest he is god-like, as these are similes for God in the Bible (for example, *II. Samuel* 32; *Psalms* 84:11), but also note words which suggest he is damaged and dangerous (for example, *ruined*). He seems very human here, and we are allowed to share in his feelings, although he seems determined to conceal them even from himself. Look at words like *followers* and *faithful*, used of the army. Does Satan's *remorse* make his continuing the war more or less forgivable?

587-8   **Thus far ... yet observed**   although these were so far above comparison, yet Satan could see them all.

594-9   **as when ... monarchs**   Epic similes comparing Satan to the sun obscured by mist or the shadow of the moon. Since God is more naturally associated with the sun, and Satan with the moon (see Approaches pp.169–70), what does the *misty air* and *dim eclipse* which change the sun's light here suggest about Satan?

595   **horizontal**   a transferred epithet (see Approaches p.161) as it is the beam, not the air, which is horizontal. Note the assonance with *Shorn* in 596.

597-9   **disastrous twilight ... monarchs**   Eclipses, like comets, were supposed to predict natural disasters and political unrest, particularly as one accompanied Christ's death (*Luke* 23:44); in what ways will Satan have this effect?

601   **thunder**   the weapon which cast him out of Heaven (see note to I 93).

601   **entrenched**   furrowed.

603   **dauntless**   fearless.

603   **considerate**   deliberate (from *considerare* (Latin), meaning to think).

606   **fellows ... followers**   one letter shifts the meaning from companion to victim.

607   Compare with I 84.

609-10   **amerced/Of Heaven**   fined or deprived of Heaven.

612-15   Epic simile comparing the army to a lightning-struck forest left standing on burnt soil (*blasted heath*); compare I 292–6 above. What does the phrase *stately growth* (referring to branches) tell you about the angels?

616-18   The main body of the army forms a close semi-circle around Satan and the other leaders (*peers*).

619   **essayed**   tried (to speak).

619   **scorn**   his own pride. Do you admire his tears or his suppression of them more?

621   **interwove**   interwoven, mixed.

Satan Gives His Army an Account of the Past and a Plan for the Future: Lines 622–69

This is Satan's first political speech and its purpose is to influence rather than inform his army, though he does tell them for the first time about Earth. What does he want them to feel, or not to feel? How does he characterize God? Do you think the complexity of the sentences suggests that Satan is hiding something?

Using the Latin terms listed at the beginning of the Notes to Book II, we can divide the speech into the following sections:

- the flattering address or **exordium** (622–3)
- the first argument or **narratio** (626–30) which attempts to explain the past, and is supported by three **confirmationes** or supporting arguments (631–4, 635–7, 637–42)
- the second narratio (643–56), which looks to the future, and is supported by one confirmatio (657–9)
- the **conclusio** summoning a council (659–62) and giving the motion for debate (what kind of war to pursue).

622	**myriads**	vast numbers (see Approaches p.148).
624	**not inglorious ... dire**	the battle was glorious even if the outcome was terrible.
625	**testifies**	witnesses, proves.
626–31		Satan's first argument (the narratio and confirmatio of 626–42) is that no-one, however prophetic or knowledge-able, could have *feared* (main verb) failure. Note how the rhetorical questions and the repeated auxiliaries (*could ... could ... can*) communicate his incredulity.
627	**presaging**	predicting.
630	**repulse**	check.
631–4	**For who ... shall fail to reascend?**	For no-one could believe they will fail to re-ascend, even though they are now (*yet*) experiencing loss. The argument that the angels, being made of fire, the lightest element, will re-ascend, is used again at II 75–6.
632	**puissant legions**	powerful divisions.

633 **emptied Heaven**   In fact (V 710) only a third of the angels were cast out.

634 **native seat**   original homeland (implying they have a right to be there).

635-7 **be witness ... our hopes**   I call all angels to vouch for the truth that it was not because I took the wrong advice, or tried to avoid dangers, that we lost. Does this absolve him of responsibility for the failure?

639-40 **old repute,/Consent or custom**   Three reasons for retaining the monarchy: its fame, its acceptance by the people, and its long history. Sneering at these means Satan has to find other reasons for justifying his own rule at II 18-21. For Milton's own contempt for monarchy, see *Approaches* pp.138-41.

640 **regal state**   royal grandeur (as opposed to practical *strength*, 641).

642 **tempted our attempt**   The pun reinforces the lie that God enticed them to attack him by appearing weak.

642 **wrought**   made, brought about.

643-56 Satan's second *narratio*. God creates the Universe after the fall of the angels (see *Approaches* p.148), but Satan says he has heard a rumour of the plan, though he prefers to see *space* as the creative force; we hear more about his plan at II 380.

644-5 **So as not ... provoked**   we will neither provoke nor respond if God provokes us (again note the characterization of God).

646-7 **to work ... effected not**   to plan secretly (*close design*) how *fraud or guile* may achieve what force failed to achieve.

648 **who overcomes ... foe**   the whole phrase is the object of *find*.

650 **rife**   prevalent.

650 **ere long**   before long (see note to 643-56).

653-4 Both here and at the next mention of Man (II 345-51) we feel Satan inflaming the jealousy of the other angels (*sons of Heaven*).

656 **eruption**   ascent (but it sounds distorted and violent).

660 **Peace is despaired** We have abandoned hope of peace (though this is not true of the angels; see II 227, 292 below).

662 **understood** one of a number of words in the speech to suggest a policy of a secret, deceitful hostility.

663 **out-flew** flew out (like *upsent* 541 above).

666 **illumined** lit up (see Approaches p.144).

666-7 **highly ... Highest** What is the effect of the pun?

668 **Clashed** A traditional Roman 'hurrah' was to clash swords on shields.

The Building of Pandæmonium: Lines 670–751

Pandæmonium is Milton's invented name for the infernal Parliament building. It is built on the model of a Greek temple, appropriate for the Classical soldiers which the angels are impersonating at the moment. It also has the ornateness which Milton may have seen in Italy in Classical-style Catholic churches such as St. Peter's cathedral in Rome. Its aesthetic values are those of Heaven; see *Revelation* 21 (quoted in Approaches p.144), where a detailed comparison is invited), but its imagery is that of a rather gross human body (*scurf, belched, womb* etc; see Approaches, pp.162-3). Is it a noble attempt to make *a Heaven of Hell* (I 255) or merely an imitation, a theatrical, temporary, empty illusion? See pictures on pp.191-3.

670 **grisly** horrifying.

674 **The work of sulphur** Sulphur (characterized by a flaky *scurf*) was supposed to be the agent which produced the other metals.

675-8 Epic simile comparing the angels to foot-soldiers (*pioneers*) preparing a battlefield; what is the effect of the comparison?

677 **Forerun** go before an army to make preparations.

678 **cast** throw up.

678 **Mammon** the Biblical personification of wealth and worldly values; see *Matthew* 6:24, *Luke* 16:13 and Approaches pp.178-9.

679 **least erected** most ignoble (he speaks last at the Council).

681 **downward bent** Directions are crucial in Milton (see Approaches p.146, p.152) for love, virtue, and creativity should always be directed towards God and not away from him or into the self.

682 **Heaven's pavement** In *Revelation* 21: 21 we are told that *the street of the [Heavenly] city was pure gold, as it were transparent glass.*

683-4 **aught divine ... vision beatific** than anything else which the angelic and mystical (*beatific*) vision was able to enjoy.

685 **men also** The Classical author Ovid saw the mining of wealth from Mother Earth as part of the fall of Man from the original Golden Age (*Metamorphosis* I 137-42), and Spenser has Mammon mining gold in Hell in *Fairie Queene* II vii (1596; see Approaches p.167).

686 **impious** irreligious, disrespectful.

686-90 **bowels, wound, ribs, ransacked the centre** more body imagery (see Approaches p.162 for the suggestion of rape).

690 **admire** wonder at.

692 **precious bane** valuable poison (an 'oxymoron', see Approaches p.161).

694 **Babel** The tower of Babel aimed to 'reach unto Heaven' (*Genesis* 11:4-9).

694 **Memphian kings** The Egyptian kings or pharaohs built the enormous pyramids near Cairo (*Memphis*); compare II 483-5.

697 **reprobate** rejected, proved bad.

697 Note here and at 711 the speed with which the edifice is built; what does this suggest to you?

700 **Nigh** nearby.

700 **cells** workshops (with underfloor furnaces).

702 **Sluiced** channelled.

703 **Founded** (*found out* in *P.L.* ed. II, 1671) melted (main verb) as in a foundry.

704 **Severing each kind and scummed the bullion dross** by their *art* or skill they separate the ores and skim the impurities (*dross*) from the pure metals (*bullion*). Or maybe *bullion dross* is another oxymoron?

705   **A third**   a third group (the first mined, the second smelted).

706-7   **A various mould ... hollow nook**   a complex mould (representing the shape of the whole building carved in reverse into the ground) into whose detailed indentations the molten metal is conveyed, by a clever system, forming a hollow shape.

708-11   Just as one expulsion of wind (*blast, exhalation*) can fill many organ pipes, so a musical breath filled the mould from underneath and blew the hollow building inside-out on top of the ground (like a plastic toy). What is suggested to you by this pneumatic building-method and sound effects (712)?

710   **Anon**   at once.

711   **exhalation**   outburst of air or wind (suggesting what?).

712   **dulcet symphonies**   sweet instrumental music. Musical proportions were supposedly allied to architectural ones, so Thebes and Troy were also constructed to the sound of music.

713-14   **pilasters round/Were set**   squared columns were arranged around (probably against the wall). See picture on p.191.

714-16   **Doric pillars ... graven**   an inner colonnade of pillars with Doric capitals (same connotations as the music at I 550) supported the golden beam (*architrave*) leading up to a projecting *cornice*, on which was carved in high relief (*bossy sculptures*) the decorative *frieze*. The architrave could go across the front or around the whole space. The effect is Classically impressive but clearly pagan.

717   **fretted**   carved in decorative patterns usually of intersecting lines, but Hamlet admired the heavens *fretted with golden fire* (II 2.313). Though the angels themselves have never seen the sky, we recognize their roof is an imitation.

717-18   **Babylon, Alcairo**   Monumental capital cities of the oppressive kingdoms of Assyria and Egypt; Babylon was in particular the focus of evil in the Bible (*Revelation* 17:5) and became an insulting name for Rome, home of the Pope. See the gigantic Assyrian sculptures in the British Museum.

720 **Belus, Serapis** the Assyrian form of Baal, and the Egyptian Osiris; see note to 419–56 and 478 above.

723 **Th'ascending pile/stood fixed** the edifice stopped rising at its proper height. In 1637 a court masque (musical entertainment) included a scene where 'the earth open'd, and there rose up a richly-adorned pallace ... with proticos vaulted, on pillasters of rich rustick work; their bases and capitels of gold. Above these ran an architrave, freese, and coronis of the same' (quoted from M. Hughes ed. of *P.L.*). In what ways is Pandæmonium like a piece of scenery?

724 **brazen folds** brass leaves.

724 **discover** reveal (but what do they reveal? compare II 890).

727 **subtle magic** clever contrivance (as opposed to God's ability to hang the stars in the sky).

728–9 **lamps ... naphtha and asphaltus** lamps containing oil from bituminous rock (*naphtha*) and hanging baskets (*cressets*) holding lumps of burning asphalt; the ingredients of Hell used to imitate the Heavenly city which *had no need of the sun, nor of the moon ... for the glory of God did light it.* (*Revelation* 23:23).

734 **sceptered angels** high-ranking angels who lived in towers.

736 **Exalted** glorified.

737 **hierarchy** his place in the hierarchy of *orders*, as in an army (see Approaches p.148. How do you respond to this glimpse of heavenly society? Does it suggest the monarchy and perhaps nobility which Milton himself had sought to overthrow (see Approaches pp.138–9). Or does it symbolize creation's ordered ascent to God (see Approaches p.146)?

739–40 **in Ausonian land ... Mulciber** in Italy (*Ausonia*) men called the Greek god Hephaestus *Mulciber* (or Vulcan). As smith and artist he built the palaces of the gods on Mount Olympus before he was thrown down by Zeus (*Iliad* I 588–95).

746 **Lemnos th'Ægæan isle** *Lemnos* in the *Ægæan* sea, where Mulciber landed.

747 **Erring** Milton claims that the story of the fall of Mulciber

is a misrepresentation of the true story of the fall of the angels (I 50-1 above; see Approaches p.148 and *Isaiah* 14:12-15 quoted p.195). Why does Milton make Mulciber sound so beautiful, and why does he emphasize this word by its position?

748   **nor aught availed**   nor did it help him.

750   **engines**   contrivances (such as the *subtle magic* of 727).

The Fallen Angels Take Possession of Pandæmonium: Lines 752-98

Having done so much to magnify and glorify the angels, Milton seems here to be using mock-epic techniques to diminish them in our eyes. A mock-epic laughs at the form and the heroic qualities of the epic (discussed in Approaches pp.167-8); Pope's *Rape of the Lock*, which is a parody of *Paradise Lost*, is an example. The passage is almost a comic interlude before the solemn business of Book II. What do the comparisons with insects (compare I 595), Pygmies, and elves suggest to you? Why does Milton have them change both their costume and their size?

753   **sovereign power**   Satan's royal power.

753   **awful**   awe-inspiring.

756   **Pandæmonium**   'All the Demons' (Milton's coinage from Greek words, which has come to mean a chaotic assembly).

758   **squared**   drawn up in a square.

759   **By place or choice the worthiest**   representatives to attend the Parliament are chosen by rank or election. Should we compare this democracy to the rigid hierarchy of Heaven (see I 737)?

763-6   Milton compares the hall to a huge crowded tent where Saracen knights were challenged (*defied*) before their sultan's (*soldan's*) throne. Saracens were the Muslim (*paynim*) opponents of the Christians in the Crusades; this continues the Romance comparisons of 579-87 above; the angels seem to have now changed their costume from that of the Classical army.

766   **career with lance**   jousting, or horseback fighting with lances.

768   Note the onomatopoeic alliteration (see Approaches p.156).

768-75   Epic simile comparing the angels to bees active in springtime (when the sun enters *Taurus* in April). Some swarm *in clusters*, others collect nectar from flowers; others walk about and discuss (*expatiate and confer*) on the plank that goes into the hive, which is rubbed with attractive oils (*balm*). Of course they only imagine they have control over *their state affairs*. How many more points of comparison can you find between the simile and the angels, and what is its effect on your attitude to them?

773   **straw-built citadel**   castle built of straw (compare the *Three Little Pigs*).

776   **straitened**   confined into too narrow a space.

777-80   The innumerable angels shrink themselves from the size of giants to tiny elves. See discussion in Approaches p.171, and compare the visual effects at I 284-95.

781   **Indian mount**   the Himalayas, beyond which the Classical historian Pliny erroneously located the pygmies, who really live in central Africa.

781-8   Epic simile comparing the diminished angels with elves. Note the care with which Milton sets the scene at night (as at I 207; see Approaches pp.169-70), when the moon provokes and witnesses (*sits arbitress*) magic and madness, and the fairies play sinister yet compelling music. How does the comparison warn us about the angels?

793-5   The chief angels (*seraphic lords*) have not diminished themselves, but sit in special seats in private council (*secret conclave*). What does this tell you about Satan's style of government?

797   **Frequent and full**   crowded and without absentees.

798   **consult**   consultation.

Notes to Book II

Synopsis to Book II: the Argument

Satan is enthroned in Pandæmonium, and formally opens the debate on the question: how should the war with God be pursued? Moloch advises they stake everything on a last attack, but Belial and then Mammon advise abandoning the war and concentrating on making Hell more comfortable. The assembly is inclined to agree with these last speakers, but Beëlzebub convinces them that they could safely continue the war through attacking God not directly, but through his new favourite, Mankind. They agree with this plan, and Satan offers to go and corrupt Man and so force God to punish him as they were punished. This offer allows the rest of the angels to stay in Hell, where they pursue a variety of amusements and also explore their new home. Meanwhile Satan searches for an escape from Hell, and finds a locked gate guarded by two terrifying monsters, a snake woman and a shadowy king. He is about to fight the latter when the woman throws herself between them and tells him they are both his children. She is Sin, born from his head when he first thought of rebelling against God, and so much a copy of Satan himself that he fell in love with her and lay with her. She was then thrown out of Heaven with Satan and the rebel angels, found herself by the gate, and given its key with the responsibility of keeping the gates locked. The other figure, Death, is their son, and the dogs which surround her are the offspring of a rape by Death upon her. Satan persuades her to open the gates, and then flies out across Chaos towards Earth. By chance he encounters its rulers, Chaos and Night, whom he also persuades to help him, by giving him directions, and the Book ends with him in sight of the world.

During the notes on the Parliament, I will be referring to the following sub-divisions of Classical speeches (see *Approaches* pp.163–5 on Milton's knowledge of these):

exordium address often naming the people addressed (and note the effect of immediacy when this is not done).

narratio statement of one argument (there can be more than one narratio).

confirmatio   evidence, proofs, arguments, and reasons for each narratio.

confutatio   refutation of objections, either imagined ones, or those raised by a previous speaker.

conclusio   a short recapitulation and proposal for action.

I will also use some of the modern and Renaissance rhetorical (speech-making) terms explained in the section on Persuasion (Approaches pp.163-7). In order to test the speeches against one another, ask the following questions about each:

Is the speaker's assessment of their situation

- true or mistaken
- a flattering delusion
- deliberately misleading?

Is his plan

- heroic or cowardly
- active or passive
- practical
- spiteful
- difficult or easy?

Satan's Elevation and Opening Speech: Lines 1–42

Satan sits like a Pope or a king in Parliament. Note all the words suggesting height (*high, exalted, uplifted*); like Pandæmonium itself he is attempting to ascend towards Heaven. This speech, like his previous one (I 622-62), is notable for his self-justification and convoluted logic. Here he is explaining why he has remained their leader in spite of the disastrous failure of his last plan. He gives four reasons for his position (*just right, fixed laws*, the angels' *free choice*, his own *merit*) but fails to mention that it was God who gave him the responsibility of leadership in the first place. Do his claims have any grounds? The implicit parallel is with Jesus, who is genuinely elevated by merit (VI 43, 758) and takes the greatest share of pain.

2-3   **Ormus ... Ind ... East**   Ormus (now Ormuz, an island town off the Persian coast), India, and the East generally were all famous for their jewels and the wealth and ostentation of their monarchs.

4 **Showers ... pearl and gold**   it was the eastern ceremony, at the coronation of their kings, to powder them with *gold-dust* and *seed-pearl* (Warburton ed. of *P.L.*).

4 **barbaric**   savage, pagan.

6 **bad eminence**   an oxymoron; is he higher or essentially lower than the others?

6-9   These lines chart Satan's psychological progress in Book I, though he cannot leave despair behind (see Approaches p.178).

8 **Beyond thus high**   beyond this point.

8 **insatiate**   ever hungry.

9 **success**   outcome (an earlier meaning); the irony of using it to mean 'failure' seems deliberate.

10 **imaginations**   fantasies.

11   This flattering exordium (see explanation above p.92) refers to two of the **orders** of angels; see Approaches p.148.

12-13   A theory expanded by Moloch II 75-81 that the *empyreal substance*, out of which the angels are made, naturally ascends and so must leave the depths (*gulf*) of Hell.

14-17   The idea that the fallen angels will have learned *celestial virtues* from their fall which will prevent a second fall, is a parody of Adam's 'fortunate fall' which taught him new virtues like humility (see Approaches p.138).

18-21   Satan argues that although he was already well-established as leader (giving the four reasons listed in the headnote), his failure has made him even more secure. Does this seem logical to you?

18 **just right**   something like the Divine Right with which Charles I vainly tried to protect his crown. For other claims, see headnote.

22 **recovered**   they are now *at least* better than they were at the beginning of Book I.

23 **unenvied**   no-one could envy his throne now, so all grant him (*yield*) his position.

28 **the Thunderer's**   God's (see note to I 93).

29 **bulwark**   defensive rampart (he is a *tower* at I 591).

32	**faction** division or intrigue within a group. Milton may be remembering the problems in the armies during the Civil War (see Approaches pp.138-9).
32-5	Satan is claiming that the upside-down nature of Hell makes his *bad eminence* one of pain, not joy, but you might think that other angels *could* envy his position.
36	**faith ... accord** faithfulness and harmony. Milton praises their *concord* (II 496-7).
37-8	Can you find two lies here? (Claiming a *just inheritance* was a standard excuse for aggressive warfare.)
39-40	This **chiasmus** (a phrase in which words reappear in reversed order, see Approaches p.166) conceals the illogicality of the argument, as *prosperity* generally does ensure one *prospers*.
41	**open war or covert guile** the motion for the debate, which assumes that the decision to continue the war has already been made. In fact this decision is what the angels actually discuss; see Approaches p.143.

Moloch's Call to Arms: Lines 43-105

Moloch was introduced as a *horrid king besmeared with blood* I 392-6 (see Approaches pp.178-9) who was both cruel and insensitive to others' pain. Though these attributes may be found in his speech, Milton says that like Satan, his thirst for revenge is grounded in *despair* because he recognizes God's genuine superiority, and his own misery in being deprived of the *bliss* of being near him. His speech is therefore essentially an appeal for mass suicide, though he presents it as a feasible plan. As befits a soldier, his style is plain, with few rhetorical figures, and no exordium, moving directly to his narratio in support of one of Satan's alternatives. It is worth distinguishing where he is truthful (for example, in his understanding of the difference between Hell and the Heaven they have lost), and where, like the other speakers, he 'packages' the truth (particularly about God).

43	**Moloch** means king.
46	**deemed** thought.
48-9	**with that care ... fear** Because he cannot be what he cares about (equality with God), he fears nothing worse.

50   **recked**   cared.

51   **sentence**   judgement.

51-2   **of wiles ... I boast not**   I do not offer suggestions for *covert guile* (41) as I am not an expert in this unmilitary field.

53   **Contrive who need**   let those who need to (which in fact include Satan) waste time in plotting rather than fighting. Note words which convey his urgency.

58   **opprobrious**   disgraceful, deserving reproach. Compare how other speakers refer to Hell, for example, II 168, 254.

60-70   Moloch's *narratio* (see explanation on p.92).

62   **resistless**   impossible to resist.

63   **horrid arms**   terrible weapons.

65   **almighty engine**   the chariot pulled by cherubim described *Ezekiel* 1:10 and used in *Paradise Lost* VI 749 by Jesus when he expels the rebel angels.

69   **Tartarean sulphur and strange fire**   *Tartarus* was the part of Hades used for punishment. Hell's mineral composition was described I 670-4; the *black fire* was mentioned in line 67 (and I 62-3).

70   As in II 64 God is seen as a sadistic inventor of torture, but the fallen angels could be said to be their real inventors; see Approaches p.180.

70   **But perhaps**   first *confutatio* or refutation of a possible objection (see explanation on p.92).

73-4   **sleepy drench/Of that forgetful lake**   Moloch suggests contemptuously that having swallowed a drink (*drench*) from the lake of fire, the angels have become lethargic and forgetful, but we will learn that they are unable to reach the waters of Lethe which might have had that effect (II 604-14).

75   **proper motion**   natural movement (see note to I 63-4) as distinct from *adverse* (77).

78   The good angels followed Satan's rebels into Chaos (*the deep*); see II 996-8.

82   **Th'event is feared**   Moloch's second *confutatio*, contradicting those who might fear the outcome (*event*) of another attack on God, which might make them *worse destroyed* (85). He answers with the rhetorical question *what can be worse?*

(85), the phrase on which Belial builds his own confutatio of Moloch.

83   **Our Stronger**   a way of referring to God which itself indicates that they cannot win.

87   **abhorred deep**   suggests the distance from *bliss* (86) as well as Moloch's hatred of Hell.

89-92   **exercise, vassals, scourge, penance**   words which suggest that Hell is a place of punishment, either one where God makes them the slaves (*vassals*) to satisfy his *wrath* and sadism, or, perhaps more flatteringly, one where religious *exercises* like scourging are accepted as penance (Fowler ed. of *P.L.*).

93   **abolished and expire**   be annihilated and die. This suggestion that the *empyreal substance* is not in fact immortal is given a terrifying imaginative construction by Belial in II 149-51 (see Approaches p.164).

94-5   **what doubt ... ire?**   why should we fear to provoke his most extreme anger?

97   **essential**   essence (see Approaches p.150).

101   **On this side nothing**   as near as we can be to nothingness, and so unable to feel (is this an admirable desire?).

101-5   Moloch's 'conclusio' returns to his original suggestion for a mass assault on Heaven, though now he hopes only to *disturb* and *alarm* an *inaccessible* God.

104   **fatal**   fated to remain.

Belial's Do-nothing Policy: Lines 106-228

Belial is so persuasive that Milton warns us directly against believing him, both before (*But all was false*) and after (*Counselled ignoble ease*). His appearance suggests a life of privilege (see his first appearance I 490-505 and Approaches pp.178-9), encouraging the vices of selfishness and slothfulness as well as *lust and violence*. But he also seems more intelligent than Moloch in his 'confutationes' of each of Moloch's points, often quoting his words: *revenge, could we . . . rise, despair, woe*, etc. He also seems more cultivated in his use of rhetoric; though his language is often simple, he can evoke with terrifying or soothing effect the possible futures open to them (see for example the analysis of 142-59 in

Approaches pp.166–7). Is he persuasive? Does he or Moloch have the more realistic understanding of their situation?

109   **act**   manner.

109   **humane**   polite.

113   **manna**   sweetness (sweets made from gum of the Manna ash were supposed to evoke the Heavenly food mentioned in *Exodus* 16 and *Psalm* 78).

113–4   Making the *worse* argument appear the *better* was associated with the logic-chopping Greek *Sophists*; the angels are compared to Greek philosophers again in II 555–65.

114   **dash/Maturest counsels**   overthrow more considered advice.

116   **To vice industrious**   an oxymoron (see Approaches p.161) suggesting the reversed values of Hell, where Belial works hard to support vice.

119   Note the relaxed, almost chatty exordium (see explanation p.92).

123   **Ominous conjecture**   possibility of things going wrong.

123   **success**   outcome (see note to II 9).

124–7   **When he ... dissolution**   When he who excels in warfare gives, as his *main reason* (121) for pursuing an aggressive revenge-policy, the fact that they will at least escape the *utter woe* of Hell by annihilation.

126   **Mistrustful**   This prominently placed word undermines the two preceding *excels* to show Moloch's lack of faith in his own powers.

127   **scope**   extent.

130   **watch**   guards.

130   **render**   make.

131   **Impregnable**   able to resist any attack.

131   **deep**   Chaos, like the *realm of Night* (133).

132   **obscure**   dark.

136   **insurrection, to confound**   uprising from Hell to defeat *Heaven's purest light* (137).

139   **th'ethereal mould**   airy form which angels were supposed to wear to make their immaterial bodies visible (see Donne *Air and Angels: And as an angel, face and wings/Of air, not pure*

as it, yet pure doth wear); it also suggests the 'form' of God himself, which cannot be corrupted or polluted.

140-2 **Incapable ... Victorious** God, unable to be stained, would purge himself of the evil (*mischief*) and inferior (*baser*) fire of Hell by victory. (Note that Hell is feminized; see Approaches pp.162-3.)

142-6 **hope/Is flat despair ... sad cure** These paradoxes (that hope is utterly devoid of hope, that the cure brings sorrow, not healing) expose the self-contradictions in Moloch's argument.

149-50 Milton's Chaos includes all the materials for creation but is itself formless (*uncreated*); see 911 below. How do you respond to the two body-imges here: *womb* and *swallowed?*

152 **Let this be good** even if we allowed that annihilation is a good.

153-4 **it** the annihilation described in 146-51, which might be incompatible with their *empyreal substance*, so that God cannot give it.

156 **belike through impotence** perhaps through lack of power (said sarcastically).

157-9 A chiasmus: the first phrase *end/Them in his anger* gives Moloch's expectation, which Belial then reverses (*whom his anger saves*) to give his own; see Approaches p.165.

160 **Say they** Do they say? (introduces another confutatio).

160-3 Contemptuously echoes 85-7. *Decreed/Reserved and destined* are all words suggesting they are fated, a suggestion which the fallen angels usually prefer (see Approaches p.177).

165 **amain** at full speed.

165 **strook** struck.

166 **besought** begged.

170 **the breath** God's breath.

173 **intermitted vengeance** interrupted (and so resumable) revenge. Satan observed I 159-77 that the angelic *ministers of vengeance* had returned to Heaven, and the *sulphurous hail* and *thunder* had stopped.

174 **red right hand** red with blood or fire; simple but terrifying words.

175 **firmamaent** sky, roof.

176-7	**cataracts ... Impendent** fiery waterfalls hanging over their heads.
179	**Designing or exhorting** planning or urging (said sarcastically).
182	**racking** torturing.
183	**yon** yonder, over there (the lake of fire).
185	**Unrespited ... unreprieved** without rest or pity or rescue. This line is scanned on p. 156.
186	**Ages of hopeless end** ages without hope of end.
187-8	Here Belial ceases his 'confutationes' and begins his 'narratio' on the motion.
190	In *De Doctrina* Milton repeats the ancient belief that God exists outside time, and so sees past, present, and future simultaneously (*at one view*); he is therefore impossible to surprise.
191	**motions** proposals.
191	**derides** scorns (echoing *Psalm* 2:4: *the Lord shall have them in derision*); God does seem to do this, for example V 718.
192	**Not more** just as.
196-7	**Better ... advice** My advice is that we should suffer these torments rather than risk worse.
197-8	**fate inevitable, omnipotent decree** unchangeable fate, all-powerful command. In contradiction to his own argument at 160-1, Belial is stressing that God has no choice but to keep them in Hell. But as we learn from the forgiveness of Adam and Eve, God never restricts his options in this way. Belial, like Satan, is trying to limit the fallen angels' choices.
199	**To suffer, as to do** As at I 158, the choice before them is seen in terms of the Classical division between acting and being acted upon (*suffering* in the archaic sense of *allowing*). Belial now has to *package* the latter option, which Milton will call *sloth* (227), as noble endurance.
199-201	**To suffer ... ordains** It is just that if we are prepared to act, we should also be prepared to accept (*suffer*) the effects of action.
201-3	**this was at first ... Contending** If we think wisely, we will realize that the present suffering was an accepted possibility (*resolved*) from the first moment we decided to fight God.

205 **venturous** daring

205 **if that fail them** if the spear fails to give them victory.

207 **ignominy** (pronounced *ignomy*) humiliation.

208 **sentence** judgement (also the meaning of *doom* 209).

210 **remit** withdraw, refrain from punishing.

211 **removed** moved far away (as in I 73 where Satan regrets what Belial here welcomes: their distance from God).

212 **us not offending** us if we do not offend (a Latinate construction).

213 **whence** therefore.

215-18 Belial suggests that their *essence* or pure nature gives grounds for hope: either it will purge off Hell-fire (as God's did at 141), or it will become used to it (*inured*) and more like it in temperament and substance (*conformed in temper and in nature*). Although this *conforming* would be a degeneration (see Approaches p.147), do you find his attitude more positive than Moloch's?

219 **void** empty.

220 Belial here is confusing the entire value system of creation as Satan did at I 160 and IV 110 (see Approaches p.178).

224 **For happy ... worst** another chiasmus; their *lot* will not be happy, but need not be the worst evil (*ill*).

Mammon Advises Building in Hell: Lines 229–83

Moloch, Belial, and Mammon have been described as 'the general, the lawyer, and the industrialist', the last being a particularly apt description of Mammon, who was introduced to us I 678–88 as a materialist even in Heaven, and who directs the mining for Pandæmonium. The second half of his speech encourages the angels to *build in Hell* (I 751), which may reflect a good desire to imitate Heaven (see Approaches p.144, p.179), or an evil desire to confuse good and evil, light and darkness (as Belial did II 220). The first part of his speech, after a quibbling philosophical introduction, does consider the unspoken question behind the debate: should they ask to return to Heaven? His answer (discussed in Approaches pp.142-3) is to sneer at the humiliation this would involve them in (a humiliation which Adam and Eve will be prepared to accept) using words which recall Milton's own dislike of monarchy (for example, *while he lordly sits*). Find also words which make their stay in Hell seem rather impressive and even *puritan* (see Approaches pp.145–6); for example, *hard liberty, our own good, useful.* What are the truths such words conceal?

229 What is the effect of the lack of exordium?

229–33 Mammon first dismisses the hope of dethroning God as being contrary to fate, which as usual in Hell is placed above God; it will only happen if chance or Chaos ruled the Universe, which they do not.

234–5 Since he has dismissed the *former* hope (of dethroning God), the *latter* hope (*regain* their lost rights to Heaven, 230) should also be dismissed, because they could have no place in Heaven if they did not first dethrone God.

236 **bound** boundary.

237–46 These lines may recall Milton's bitterness in 1660, when England gave up its new-found liberty and restored the monarchy. Charles II did *publish grace to all* by issuing a general pardon which included an expectation of future obedience (*on promise made/Of new subjection*); see headnote.

239–40 **with what eyes could we/Stand?** How would we have the face to stand?

243 **Forced hallelujahs** enforced words of praise (such as the blessed sing in *Revelation* 19:1).

244–6 **breathes ... servile offerings** gives off the perfume of the Heavenly food (*ambrosia*) we present to him (though in the description of Heaven in the next book, the ambrosia comes from God, see III 185). Mammon is 'packaging' the worship of God as slavish; compare what Satan says about it in his soliloquy (pp.177–8; see Approaches p.164 on 'packaging').

249 Note how this 'imaginative construction' of their return ends in the word *hate*.

249–54 **Let us not ... ourselves** Let us not seek our former Heavenly state of splendid slavery (*vassalage*), which is impossible to obtain by force, and too humiliating to obtain by God's consent, but live independently from our own resources.

254 **vast recess** euphemism for Hell; compare Moloch's name for it at II 58.

256-7 **Hard liberty, easy yoke** difficult liberty (is preferable to) easy responsibilities. Is Milton putting much of his own preference for liberty into Mammon's mouth (see Approaches p.142)? Beëlzebub dismisses this *liberty* (II 316-21). The *yoke* (burden) may be meant to recall Jesus's offer to the heavy-laden *For my yoke is easy* (*Matthew* 11:28-30).

260 **We can create** main verb; the preceding adjectives (*useful ... adverse*) show what kind of positive *things* can be created from their opposites, so demonstrating the angels' power to overcome difficulties like the Puritan colonists of the New World.

262 This puritan plea for *labour* and *endurance* is somewhat contradicted by his next promise of comforts.

264 **Sire** Lord.

266 **majesty of darkness** see *Psalm* 18:11-13: '*his pavilion round about him was dark waters and thick clouds ... The Lord also thundered in the heavens.*

268 **Mustering** gathering together.

271 **Wants not her hidden lustre** does not lack (archaic meaning of *want*, as at 272) her hidden brightness; the feminine pronoun recalls I 685 when mining is a kind of rape.

275 **elements** materials out of which we are made (instead of the angelic ether; see note to II 139). Devils were supposed to be made of Hell-fire, and Mammon, like Belial 215-20, welcomes this transformation.

276 **temper** temperament (the balance of the *humours* in seventeenth-century science).

277-8 **needs remove ... pain** must necessarily kill those too sensitive to pain. In fact Satan, who feels their woe most keenly, does not die but degenerates.

280 **order** See Approaches p.147 on the chaos this conceals.

281 **Compose** organize.

The Response of the Fallen Angels and Description of Beëlzebub: Lines 284–309

The relieved applause of the angels at hearing two of their princes advise peace after the storms and *thunder* of their recent battle, is clearly not what Satan wanted or expected to hear. His motion had only invited contributions on the method of continuing their war with God, but Belial and Mammon have advised ending the war altogether. That Beëlzebub and Satan now combine to reverse the angels' 'decision' demonstrates how false are promises of free choice in Hell. The passage also gives us our first description of Beëlzebub, who like Satan (I 593) retains a strong resemblance to the unfallen archangels (see Approaches p.179).

286–90   This epic simile, comparing the applause to the sound of a dying storm, is discussed in Approaches p.157. The deep-sea music (*hoarse cadence*) after a storm soothes the over-tired (*o'erwatched*) sailors in their small boat (*bark … or pinnace*); the fallen angels too are recovering from a storm.

294   **Michael**   The archangel who led God's army (VI 250).

292   **field**   battle.

295   **Wrought still**   continued to work away.

296   **nether empire**   lower kingdom (dismissed by Beëlzebub, 378).

297   Compare 221–2 above.

298   **In emulation opposite**   in rivalry and in opposition (like the temples to the pagan gods described I 400–3).

301   **Aspect**   expression.

302   **A pillar of state**   a main support of the state.

302   **on his front engraven**   (lines) etched into his forehead.

303–4   The qualities of thoughtfulness, care for the ordinary subject, and the ability to advise princes, are half-personified as presiding over his mind – or at least his features. His intelligence is clear from his speech.

305   **sage**   wise.

306   **Atlantean**   like those of Atlas (the Titan who supported the sky as a punishment for rebelling against Zeus). Again his appearance, not his nature, is being described.

307   **look**   gaze (presumably stern).

Beëlzebub's Proposal and the Angels' Response: Lines 310–89

Beëlzebub begins by demolishing the peaceable arguments of Belial and Mammon, echoing their words contemptuously (*thus far removed, peace, doing, and suffering*) and dismissing their hopes as fantasies (*dreams, projecting*). He is closer in spirit to Moloch's understanding of Hell as a *dark opprobrious den of shame*, and also urges the necessity of seeking *revenge*. However (and here he does agree with Belial and Mammon), he does not see any point in a *dangerous expedition* against Heaven itself, and so proposes the plan which Satan had introduced at I 650–6: to go to Earth and corrupt Mankind (see Approaches p.150. How does he inflame the fallen angels' jealousy and appeal to their cowardice?

310–11	Note the flattering exordium, violently reversed at 313 with the prominently-placed *Princes of Hell* (sneering at their *nether empire*, 296).
312	**style** title.
317	**dungeon ... safe retreat** With which previous speakers would you associate either of these descriptions of Hell?
318–20	**Beyond his arm, to live exempt, in new league** Three phrases which ironically elaborate on the supposed *safe retreat*: out of God's reach, outside his law, or in a confederacy *against* his rule.
320	**but** introduces what he really thinks (that God has *doomed* or condemned them permanently).
321	**thus far removed** a contemptuous quotation from Belial's speech (211).
321–2	**bondage, curb** words used for restraining animals. What does this imply about the fallen angels?
322	**reserved** preserved (he suggested in I 149 that they were enslaved to serve God).
324	This recalls Biblical phrases about the universal presence and the eternity of God, from *Romans* 8:39: *Nor height nor depth ... shall be able to separate us from the love of God*, and *Revelations* 1:11: *I am ... the first and the last*).

327 **His empire** contrasting with *nether empire* (296) and *growing empire* (315).

327-8 **iron sceptre ... golden** harsh or mild rule (see *Revelation* 2:27: *he shall rule them with a rod of iron*).

329 **What sit we then projecting peace and war?** Why do we sit here scheming? (*projection* was associated with the delusive science of alchemy; see also *dream* 315).

330 **determined** ended (from Latin *terminare*: to terminate).

330 **foiled** frustrated (also following *war*).

331-2 **terms ... sought** for peace has been neither offered (*vouchsafed*) by God or *sought* by us. This is said against Belial's proposal at 279.

333-4 **Custody, stripes, arbitrary punishment** all words suggesting penal injustice (imprisonment, whippings, wilful punishments).

336 **to our power** to the limit of our power.

337 **Untamed reluctance** uncontrolled resistance.

339 **how the Conqueror least/May reap his conquest** a chiasmus (pivoting on *may* because *least* and *reap* echo each other's vowels) suggesting how the angels can reverse God's plans, or at least frustrate his sadistic enjoyment; compare I 164 where Satan speaks of *perverting* God's ends.

340 **doing, suffering** Beëlzebub takes up Belial's distinction (199), but insists that now the *doing* is all on God's side, and consists in inflicting *suffering* on the fallen angels. All they can do is to prevent him rejoicing in it (compare 371 below).

341 **Nor will occasion want** Nor shall we lack occasions (are these to be military ones?).

346-7 Since Satan was expelled *before* the creation of the world and Man, Milton invents this Heavenly rumour about its future occurrence (*prophetic fame*) in order that Satan should be informed about them; see also I 651-4.

347 **seat** residence.

348 **about this time** The world must have been created during the nine days Satan and his angels have been lying in the fiery lake, because Satan makes a journey to it at the end of Book II.

349　**like to us**　Both angels and Man are made in the image of God; see *Psalm* 8:5: *Thou has made him a little lower than the angels, and hast crowned him with glory and honour.*

352-3　**oath,/That shook**　From *Isaiah* 13:12-13: *I will make a man ... Therefore I will shake the Heavens*, though if Beëlzebub heard the oath why does he mention the rumour?

354　**Thither ... thoughts**　Let us concentrate our thoughts on that place.

355-6　**mould/Or substance**　form or material (see 139 above).

356　**how endued**　supplied with what qualities.

357　**attempted**　attacked (Fowler notes the pun on *tempt*, the method actually chosen).

359　**Arbitrator**　Judge. The fallen angels always manage to avoid calling him 'God'.

360　**exposed**　Note how the word is itself *exposed* at the end of the line.

362　**who hold it**　of those who tenant it (Adam and Eve).

364　**onset**　attack; he suggests three methods: devastation, expulsion, and corruption.

367　**puny habitants**　weak inhabitants (with a pun on its archaic meaning: newborn).

368　**Seduce them to our party**　persuade them to betray God and join us. (Satan will do this by enticing them to eat the fruit of the forbidden tree, but at this point only the policy, not the precise plan, has been formulated.)

369-70　**repenting hand/Abolish his own works**　God nearly does do this with the Flood, according to *Genesis* 7:7: *I: will destroy ... both man and beast, ... for it repenteth me that I have made them.*

371-2　**interrupt ... confusion**　spoil his triumph at our fall, the aim which Beëlzebub had given them 337-40. He substitutes *our joy ... In his disturbance*, the familiar policy of frustrating God which Satan introduced I 162-5.

373　**darling sons/Hurled headlong**　God's new children, Mankind, will be expelled from Paradise exactly as Satan was from Heaven in I 45; why does Milton repeat the phrase and what do you feel about Mankind suffering precisely the same fate as the fallen angels?

374   **partake with us**   share our punishment.

375   **frail originals**   Adam and Eve, the weak parents of the rest of Mankind. Beëlzebub hopes all Mankind will be punished for Adam's *original* sin, as indeed they are, for eating the fruit *brought death into the world* and Eve in particular was *cursed* for this (I 3; see Approaches p.150).

375-6   **faded ... Faded**   At one of the saddest moments in the poem, when Adam sees that Eve has eaten the fruit, he drops a garland he had made for her, and *all the faded roses shed* (IX 893); this is when decay first enters Paradise.

378   **Hatching**   plotting (with a sneer at Moloch's plans for improving Hell, 273).

379-80   Satan first suggested it to the angels I 650-6, though we can suppose he has discussed it in more detail with Beëlzebub.

382-3   **confound ... in one root**   ruin the entire race by ruining its ancestor (Adam).

383-4   We see the beginning of the mingling of Hell with Earth at the end of Book II, when a bridge is built between them along which Death and the devils pass.

384   **spite**   a word particularly associated by Milton with Satan's revenge misdirected on to the easier target of Mankind.

386   **His glory to augment**   to increase God's glory (by forgiving and restoring fallen Mankind).

387   **states**   ranks in Parliament.

389   **They vote**   Is the democracy an illusion, or are they really free and united?

Beëlzebub Asks for Volunteers and the Angels' Response: Lines 390–429

Beëlzebub expresses his pleasure at the angels' decision by flattering them, and by elaborating on the pleasures in store for them in Earth (see Approaches pp.164–5) on his advertisement of Earth's amenities). His request for a volunteer mimics God's similar request in Book III for a volunteer to save Mankind:

'Say Heavenly powers, where shall we find such love
Which of ye will be mortal to redeem
Man's mortal crime? ...
He ended, but all the Heavenly choir stood mute   (III 213–17)

Finally, Jesus offers to make the journey to Earth, because only he has sufficient love to accept Adam's punishment of death in his place. Like God, Beëlzebub mentions the qualities necessary for the journey, though in his case they include not *love* but *strength, art, evasion*. Is he exaggerating the difficulties of the journey and if so, why? Do you think Satan is genuinely *of highest worth* (429) in daring to go?

391	**Synod** council.
391	**like** (you have judged) according to your true status as gods. Contrast his previous 'exordium' (313).
394–5	**ancient seat, bright confines** their birthright, the bright regions of Heaven.
395–6	**neighbouring, opportune** their proximity to Heaven might offer opportunities for attack.
397	**mild zone** temperate region.
398	**not unvisited** a double negative, therefore *visited*. In fact the light on Earth comes from the sun, not Heaven (though all light imitates the divine light).
399	**orient** from the East (or more simply, brilliant).
400	**Purge** Beëlzebub is applying Belial's description (II 141) of how God would cleanse himself of Hell, to the angels themselves.
404	**Sufficient** fit.
404	**tempt** attempt.
404	**wandering** see Approaches pp.179–80.
405	**unbottomed** limitless. Chaos, which would have to be crossed to reach Earth, has some of the associations of outer space.
406	**palpable obscure** almost touchable darkness (compare I 63 and see Approaches pp.161–2).
407	**uncouth** unknown and rough.
408	Note the concentration of unstressed, flapping syllables in *indefatigable* (undaunted; see Approaches p.155).

409 **abrupt** precipitousness (see Satan's fall II 933); the rhythm evokes the sense.

409-10 **arrive/The happy isle** arrive at Earth (here associated with the Islands of the Blessed of Greek myth).

412 **stations thick** pockets close together (like stars, suggests Broadbent).

413-15 **Here he had ... suffrage** he will need here the ability to look around him and we will need careful choice in our election.

416 **weight** responsibility.

418 **suspense** suspended.

419 **second** support.

420 **mute** silent; its position at the end of the line is repeated III 217 (see headnote).

424 **Heaven-warring** warring on Heaven.

425 **So hardy as to proffer** So daring as to offer to go.

428 **monarchal pride** kingly pride, contrasting with Jesus's *meek* offer III 266.

Satan Offers to Journey to Earth: Lines 430–66

We see two sides to Satan here: he is undoubtedly heroic and self-sacrificing in undertaking a journey with difficulties he anticipates fairly accurately (see II 629-1055); and yet he also seems manipulative, making use of his heroism to consolidate his position (445-56). When praising himself, his grammar is very convoluted, suggesting a dubious argument. From 456 he gives the angels new instructions, which show his awareness of their different desires; some are to retain their military occupation and guard Hell; some are to try to make it more comfortable; no-one is to accompany him. Having taken the burden of revenge, he has left them to *peaceful sloth* (227). Why does he end so abruptly?

430 **progeny** race.

430 **empyreal thrones** Heavenly kings.

431 **demur** doubt.

432   **undismayed**   he is flattering them; see I 422.

432-3   In *Aeneid* VI the Sibyl explains that the journey down to the Underworld is easy, but it is extremely difficult to get back.

434   **convex of fire**   dome of fire (as at I 298 and II 635).

435   **Outrageous to devour**   immoderately hungry to eat us (see picture p.192).

435   **immures**   walls.

436   **Ninefold**   The Styx circles Vergil's Underworld nine times, but Satan finds at II 646-7 that only the gates of Hell have nine thicknesses (*ninefold*) of which only three are of the fabulous impregnable rock *adamant*.

437   **egress**   exit.

438-41   **void profound, wide gaping, abortive gulf**   phrases which support Belial's nightmare vision (II 150) of a *wide womb of uncreated night*. How do these additional body words (*gaping* or yawning, *abortive*) suggest undoing of creation and dissolution? In fact Chaos will turn out to be anything but a void.

439   **unessential night**   formlessness and darkness of Chaos (see Approaches p.181).

442   **scape**   escape.

443   **what remains him less**   what remains for him apart from.

445   **ill become**   not be worthy of.

447-50   **if aught ... attempting**   if anything judged of public importance, should, because of its difficulty or peril, deter me from performing it.

451-6   **and not refuse ... honoured sits?**   why do I agree (*not refuse*) to reign if I will not accept danger as well as honour? He who reigns must expect as his *due* more danger (*hazard*) for every increase in honour. Is Milton deliberately making Satan over-subtle and convoluted?

457   **intend at home**   occupy yourselves as if at home.

461   **respite, deceive, slack**   give a break from, cheat, or lessen the pain. How do you see this task?

462   **ill mansion**   evil place where they must remain (from Latin *manere*, see I 268).

462   **intermit no watch**   set an uninterrupted watch.

The Conclusion of the Council:
Lines 466–505

Although Milton does give the angels some negative aspects here (their disinclination for danger, or their idolatrous worship of Satan), he also praises them. Satan's unselfishness (481–2), and their general unity (497) contrast unfavourably with human behaviour, and even when men show an occasional virtue, they should remember that even devils can do as much, and curb their pride in themselves. The same point was made about the building of Pandæmonium (I 695). Should we really admire these aspects of the fallen angels? The idea that they have become devils, a word used of them for the first time at 496, united in an organized campaign of tempting humans (505) is medieval, and perhaps a bit folksy. You may prefer to believe Milton means it allegorically: the *hellish foes* (504) are inside our own minds.

466	As in a Parliament, a king's rising signifies the end of the session and so *prevented all reply*.
468	**from his resolution raised** their courage raised by his resolute example.
470	**erst** before (when there was a chance they might be accepted).
472–3	**winning ... earn** earning the reputation (for courage and self sacrifice) simply by offering to go; Satan made a similar link between *honour* and *hazard* at 453.
473–5	**they ... forbidding** they were as afraid of his disapproval as of the journey.
478	**With awful reverence prone** bending low with awe and reverence.
483–5	'which should prevent bad men from boasting of their superficial achievements (which are stirred by the desire for glory) or their industrious virtue (*zeal*) which – below the attractive surface – promotes their secret ambitions.'
486	**doubtful consultations** problematic issues raised by the debate.
488–95	Epic simile comparing the change in the angels' mood to a change in the weather: stormy in the morning (488–91), sunny in the evening (492–5).

489   **Ascending**   coming from the mountain.

490   **louring element**   frowning sky.

497   **Firm concord**   faithful agreement.

498-9   **Of creatures ... peace**   in spite of being rational, and having the hope of God's mercy, because they live after Christ's birth, when the angels proclaimed peace on Earth (see *Luke* 2: 14 and Approaches pp.150-1).

501   **levy**   raise up.

502   **Wasting**   destroying, laying waste.

503-4   **As if ... besides**   As if he did not have enough (*enow*) foes already from Hell, which might persuade us to unite with one another.

Games and Arts in Hell: Lines 506-69

The debate ends with the kind of ostentatious ceremony Milton might have associated with monarchy. We are then offered a relaxing episode after the intensity of the debate: first (a) a description of athletic games (528-45, a traditional episode in epic narrative; see Approaches p.172); then (b) the sorrowful singing of an epic about their own situation (546-51), and finally (c) a philosophical debate (555-69). Do you admire these activities, as examples of the fallen angels' culture and resourcefulness? Or do you pity them as futile, self-deceptive, expressing a lack of purpose and direction? It may help you to list words suggesting falsity and imitation (for example, *alchemy* 517, *vain*, *false* 565) and words suggesting the wandering and restless characteristic of Hell (for example, *in wandering mazes lost* (561); these are discussed in Approaches pp.179-80). How much are they following Satan's advice to find a *cure or charm* (460) for their pain?

506   **Stygian**   Underworld (the Styx was the river which encircled the Greek Underworld).

508   **paramount**   overlord.

509-10   **nor less/Than**   as great as (but under the inverted value-system of Hell, to be the greatest is to be the worst; see 29-30).

511   **imitated**   artificial and spurious, but perhaps also revealing

Satan's persistent memory of Heaven, as described in III 583.

512 **globe of fiery seraphim**   a sphere of that group of fallen angels originally connected with fire (from Hebrew *seraph*, meaning to burn), imitating God in III 583.

513 **emblazonry**   heraldic decorations.

513 **horrent**   bristling (see note to I 224).

514-15 They proclaim the result of their session to the lower angels who were not present at the *secret conclave* (I 795), explaining it by heralds (518).

517 **alchemy**   alloy used in cheap trumpets (as Broadbent observes, in *1 Corinthians* 13:1 even the *tongue of angels* becomes *sounding brass and tinkling cymbal* if it lacks love).

520 **acclaim**   shouted applause.

522 **presumptuous**   unduly confident, arrogant.

522 **ranged**   in ranks.

523 **Disband**   are dismissed.

526 **Truce**   peace (see headnote on *wandering restlessness*).

(a) Athletic games: 528-46

528 **sublime**   raised up.

529-38 The *Olympian* games in honour of Apollo (the *Pythian* god) would also have comprised races (528-9 – though not in the air) and horseback and chariot races (531-2), though the tournaments (532) are more associated with medieval games.

529 **contend**   compete.

530 **fields**   contests.

531 **shun the goal**   avoid hitting the turning post in chariot races.

532 **fronted brigads**   teams of warriors facing one another.

533-8 Epic simile comparing the games to stormy skies, thought on Earth to precede political disturbance for *proud cities*; see also the *disastrous twilight* of I 597.

535 **van**   front rank, vanguard.

536-8 **Prick fórth ... burns**   The clouds appear like knights who ride (*prick forth*) towards each other until enclosed by the masses of the opposing cloudy army; the lightning (which makes the whole sky or *welkin* burn) looks like their pointed lances.

539-40 **vast Typhoean rage more fell/Rend up** They tear up hills with the more dangerous rage of Typhus. He is the hundred-headed Titan mentioned at I 199 who, with his brothers, hurled hills at Zeus in revolt (see Approaches p.169). His name means *whirlwind*. The good angels also tore up hills when enraged by the rebel angels' cannon (VI 644-5).

542 Epic simile comparing the fallen angels to Hercules (*Alcides*) who, according to Ovid (*Metamorphosis* 9), was presented with a poisoned (*envenomed*) robe on his return from *Oechalia* when he had killed King Eurytus. Unable to remove it, and maddened with pain, he tore up pine trees to make his own funeral pyre, and threw the innocent *Lichas* (545), who had brought it, from Mount Oeta into the sea.

(b) Music and song: 446-55

549 **hapless** unlucky; note the number of words here with this meaning.

550 **By doom of battle** by judgement of battle (and therefore unjust).

550-1 **and complain ... chance** They lament that fate (the deterministic force they have substituted for God) has made the possession of virtue or strength a matter of chance. In fact, God protects *free virtue*, including theirs (see Approaches p.138, p.177).

552 **partial** prejudiced in their favour, and also 'written in parts' (Fowler ed. of *P.L.*).

554 **Suspended Hell** riveted the attention of the inhabitants of Hell, and also interrupted their pain, as Orpheus' song had suspended pain in the Underworld (Vergil *Georgias* iv 481-4, Prince); music was given the same power at I 556-9.

(c) Philosophy: 555-69

556 Eloquence charms the soul, as music charms the senses; both therefore provide the *cure or charm* which Satan had

commanded them to find at 460, though there seems an element of self-deception in both.

559-61   **Of providence ... lost**   They first discuss the philosophical conflict between God's foreknowledge or plan (*Providence*), which appears to rob his creatures of *free will*. Since the fallen angels prefer to be fatalistic (see 550-1 above and headnote), they find no way out of the problem, and keep repeating words (see Approaches p.146 on *wandering*).

562-5   This moral discussion concerns Stoic *apathy* or rejection of all *passion*, including *happiness*, *misery*, the desire for *glory*, and the dread of *shame*. This philosophy has its nobility, but one can imagine it appealing merely to the *peaceful sloth* (227) of the fallen angels. Milton, brought up in the Christian tradition of salvation through suffering, rejects it as *vain wisdom*.

566   **sorcery, charm**   As at 556 above these words recall Satan's instructions to the angels at 460 (see headnote); to discuss philosophy without allowing it to change behaviour cannot *cure* their situation, but it can *charm* it.

568-9   **Fallacious hope ... steel**   Because their hope of finding real relief is false (*fallacious*), their willingness to endure pain (*patience*) or to harden their hearts (*th'obdured breast*) can only protect them *for a while* (567). The strength and hardness associated with *arm, steel* etc., suggest both Milton's respect for Stoic patience, and his preference for the Christian patience of the suffering and compassionate Christ.

The Exploration of Hell: Lines 570-628

The final occupation which the angels give themselves is to explore Hell. How much do you admire, and how much pity them as they confront the full horror of their situation? Do they seem to be surveying rather than experiencing the pains of Hell? Notice words which continue the search for a numbing effect, such as that offered by music or philosophy (for example, *sweet forgetfulness*, 608). The infernal geography is taken not only from epic literature (particularly Dante's

Inferno xxxi–xxxiv, where there is also an ice-landscape), but also from actual travellers' accounts. But Milton has given it a characteristic emotional dimension. Because he followed St. Augustine in conceiving of evil as the negation of goodness and life, Hell is a place of perversions and anti-life. Its creations are distortions, monsters; its language is full of oxymorons and paradoxes (*where all life dies*); and the damned live only to suffer and be tantalized by their experience of deadness and numbness. Once again physical and emotional words are mixed together (for example, *region dolorous*, 619), and again the angels find *no rest* (618). Can you find emotional equivalents for these physical tortures (for example, the gnawing of remorse and regret)? See Approaches p.162, p.172 where the passage is compared with Vergil (Appendix, pp.196-7).

570 **gross** keeping close together.

572 **clime** region (as in I 242).

574 **flying march** They travel by wing (though possibly by foot as well).

575-81 **four infernal rivers** The names of the rivers are taken from Aeneid vi; Milton translates them, for *Styx* derives from *hate*, *Acheron* from *woe*, *Cocytus* from *wailing*, and *Phlegeton* from *flaming* (Prince). All therefore suggest and incite evil (*baleful*), emotions even *Phlegeton*, which is flowing (*torrent*) with rage as well as fire.

582 **Far off** Lethe does not empty itself (*disgorge*, 575) into the lake.

583 **Lethe** means *forgetting*. To drink it would intensify the numbing effect of the music (586 is very like I 558) or of Stoic philosophy just described at 568-9), so *the damned* will be tortured by being denied it (605-14).

584 **labyrinth** maze, suggesting a slow-moving river delta. Why is this emotionally appropriate for *forgetting*?

587 **flood** river.

588 **beat** beaten.

590-1 **gathers heap ... ancient pile** the unthawed snow and hail piles up like an ancient ruin. Milton may be remembering here the genuine description of polar exploration written by the sixteenth-century traveller, Sir Hugh Willoughby.

117

592   **gulf profound, Serbonian bog**   The infernal snowfields are not frozen but form a yielding pit, like the *Serebonian* bog in the Nile delta (near the city of *Damieta* and south of *Mount Cassius*) which according to the explorer Sandys looked deceptively like dry sand and so trapped 'whole armies' (Verity ed. of *P.L.*). How can this comparison be read (as an epic simile) on two levels?

595   **frore**   freezing (this paradoxical cold fire is typical of Hell).

596   **by harpy-footed Furies haled**   dragged by claw-footed goddesses (the Furies came from the Underworld to enact vengeance in Greek myths).

597   **revolutions**   repeated times.

597   **all the damned**   Is Milton writing of the human souls who will be tortured in Hell, or the fallen angels themselves, whose *ethereal warmth* (601) will feel cold acutely (such as that of becoming snakes, which they suffer at regular intervals; X 575)? Whoever it is, it seems to be in the future.

598-9   This *bitter change* from cold to heat to cold is accentuated by the chiasmus (see Approaches p.165).

600   **starve**   be numbed or 'dead' with cold. Again there seems a parallel with the numbing effects of music and philosophy (see note to 583).

601   **ethereal warmth**   the celestial fire from which spirits and souls are made.

604   **Lethean sound**   the cold and hot regions appear to be divided by a narrow stretch (*sound*) of the river Lethe, over which the *damned* will be ferried. This passage still seems to be set in the future.

605   **augment**   increase.

610   **fate withstands**   their fate (punishment) prevents them from drinking from Lethe.

611   To see *Medusa*, the worst of the *Gorgons* (female monsters with claws and snakes instead of hair), would turn one to stone, again a numbing image.

613   **wight**   person.

614   **Tantalus**   mythical king condemned to stand in the Underworld river Cocytus whose waters fled from his thirsty lips.

614 **Thus roving on** After the passage set in the future (596–614), we now return to the present and the exploration of Hell.

616 **aghast** appalled.

618–19 **No rest ... region dolorous** See headnote for the philosophical and emotional geography here.

621 A line beginning with three dragging **spondees** (see Approaches p.155).

622–3 Does this line contradict Milton's repeated insistence that only Satan or Man, not God, can create evil (see Approaches p.180)? Or do you feel this landscape is *only good* because it is an instrument of just punishment?

625 **prodigious** unnatural.

627 **Than fables ... conceived** than those inadequately suggested by fables or one's own fears.

628 **Gorgons, Hydras, Chimeras** fantastic monsters; for *Gorgons* see note to 611; *Hydra* was a many-headed snake; a *Chimera* any creature composed of parts of other creatures.

Satan Encounters Sin and Death:
Lines 629–80

Milton's inventiveness reaches new heights in this passage, which brings to life the Christian belief that death is a result of sin (see Approaches pp.180–1). At this point, however, neither Satan nor we know the names or understand the psychological and moral implications of these characters, and it is Satan's courage in confronting his first real challenge since his fall which is most striking (677–80). Milton models the woman, *Sin*, on two allegorical female monsters: Spenser's Error (*Fairie Queene* I 14), also a snake below the waist, and the mythical *Scylla* (*Aeneid* iii 424), who gave birth to dogs. Such myths might suggest fear of female sexuality, though Sin herself seems to be a victim rather than an aggressor, figuratively raped by the dogs who *kennel* in her womb (658). The *other shape*, *Death*, emerges not from Classical sources, but from medieval pictures of King Death with his spear, and from those human fears of darkness, extinction, and shapelessness which Belial had exploited in his speech. Milton intensifies the atmosphere of horror by his epic similes (see Approaches pp.169-70).

630 **highest design** ambitious purpose.

631 **Puts on swift wings** flies fast (not a new pair!).

632 **explores** tests, finds the way for.

633 **He scours** he searches.

633-4 **coast, deep** perhaps the edge of the burning lake.

634 **shaves** skims.

635 **fiery concave** roof vaulted with fire (I 298, see also 434).

635 **touring high** circling.

636-42 Epic simile comparing Satan to a spice-fleet, which although actually sailing *close* before the trade winds at the Equator (*aequinoctial*), appears to be suspended in the sky. Such fleets brought spices and medicines (*drugs*) from Bengal and the Spice Islands *Ternate* and *Tidore* in the Indonesean archipelago, on the merchant route (*trading flood*) towards the South Pole, round the Cape of Good Hope, and back towards England. How many points of comparison can you find between Satan and the fleet (look at the mirage, the journey, the cargo, and its effect on the purchaser)?

641 **wide Ethiopian** broad ocean off Ethiopia.

642 **Ply stemming nightly** Tack their way at night (as Satan is doing).

644 **Hell's bounds ... roof** the walls of Hell meeting the roof which bristles with fire.

645-6 This was anticipated by Beëlzebub II (436-7), though he said all nine thicknesses were adamant.

647 **impaled** fenced (but not consumed by) fire.

652 **Voluminous and vast** with numerous heavy coils (note the alliteration).

653 **mortal** deadly (the opposite way round from *I Corinthians* 15:56: *The sting of death is sin*).

654 **cry** pack.

655 **Cerberean** like Cerberus, the three-headed dog who guarded Hades.

656   **peal**   the baying of hounds; unending barking was one of the tortures of Dante's *Inferno*.

659–66   Epic similes comparing Sin's dogs to those associated with Scylla (see headnote) and Hecate. Scylla was a nymph who was made to give birth to dogs by Circe, aided by Hecate, Queen of the witches, who was supposed to ride through the air followed by dogs, and who also held a key (see 725 below).

660–1   **the sea ... shore**   the straits which separate *Calabria* in Italy from the murmuring beach of Sicily (*Trinacria*). This is where Scylla was supposedly turned into a dangerous rock.

662   **night-hag**   Hecate; see note to 659–66.

664   **infant blood**   murdered children were supposedly used in witches' spells.

665–6   The long nights of Lapland were thought to attract witches powerful enough to eclipse the moon (which supposedly *laboured* when eclipsed, though the word might also refer to its changing shape). The fallen angels were also associated with the moon and witchcraft (I 781–8), and Satan with eclipses (I 597).

667–70   **If shape ... either**   It had no clear body either in shape, limbs, or material, for *substance* and *shadow* seemed to be like one another. Hell is a place of contradictions and nightmare.

668   **member**   part.

671   **Furies**   see note to 596 above; notice the alliteration in these frightening lines about Death (666–73).

672   **dart**   spear.

673   **crown**   see *Revelation* 6:2: *a crown was given [Death], and he went conquering.*

676   **horrid**   causing horror.

677   **Th'undaunted ... admired**   Satan was unafraid, but wondered what this might be. Does this show courage, or simply an inability to fear (see Approaches p.174)?

678–9   **God ... nor shunned**   he only truly valued or feared God and Jesus (who was not *created* but begotten). Does this suggest an uncaring, nihilistic basis to his courage, reminiscent of Moloch (II 48–9)?

121

Sin Prevents the Battle between Satan and Death: Lines 681–745

We learn here of Satan's genuine feelings about these characters; note the contrast between the words he uses here (such as *execrable*, *detestable*) and the *smooth* words he uses later to Sin after 815. We are also shown aspects of his character besides courage: for example, arrogance (683) and determination (684). Death seems equally proud (as he was traditionally characterized), and there is an almost comic debate between them about who has the highest rank (Death was only born in Hell, but he believes himself king) whose irony is revealed when Sin tells them they are father and son. She tells them that the real battle will be between both of them and Jesus, but the drama of this near battle makes the epic more exciting and more Classical. Do you think it appropriate that Death appears (for example, at 699–700) to express God's point of view? Why does Milton consistently refuse to name Death, using instead words like *goblin* and *grisly terror*?

681   **execrable**   accursed, abhorrent.

683   **Thy miscreated ... way**   your misshapen face across my way; note the arrogance in this.

686   **taste thy folly**   realize it was folly by its effects.

687   **Hell-born**   Satan guesses right (see 782).

691   **Unbroken**   The peace and loyalty (*faith*) were whole before Satan's rebellion.

692   This shows Satan was exaggerating at I 633.

693   **Conjured**   conspired (from Latin *jurare*, meaning to swear).

696   **spirits of Heaven**   He and Sin have not been punished and so consider (*reckon*) themselves still Heavenly.

700   Death presumes Satan is fleeing the pains of Hell, and tells him to return faster than he came (*add wings*).

704   **grisly**   causing horror.

705   Because Death has no definite shape, it cannot be contained, and its growth threatens to absorb those near it (his *famine* of 847 below). Satan also grows, becoming more fiery (708).

707-8   **indignation, Unterrified**   a similar contrast to 677 above, with the word describing his lack of fear again placed at the beginning of a line.

708-11   Epic simile comparing Satan to a comet which appeared in 1618 in the northern constellation of *Ophiucus* or 'serpent-holder' (suggesting he is equivalent to Death with his *whip of scorpions* 701). Comets with tails (*horrid hair*) like the *eclipse* (*666*) supposedly brought disasters.

712   Satan also seems to be armed with a spear.

714-18   Epic simile comparing the encounter with that of storm clouds which, like eclipses or comets, also presaged disaster (see II 533-8). Note the onomatopoeic effects of repetitions, particularly *t*.

715   **With heaven's artillery fraught**   laden with lightning and thunder.

716   **Caspian**   The Caspian sea was supposedly subject to storms.

718   It was believed that thunder was caused by the crashing together of storm clouds; see II 538 above.

721   **but once more**   referring to Jesus' descent into Hell to bind Satan and release Mankind. He had overcome Death by dying on the Cross; see *Hebrews* 2:14 and Approaches p.150.

723   **Had been**   would have been.

723   **rung**   resounded.

725   **fatal key**   the keys of our fate. She is the opposite of St. Peter, who holds the keys to Heaven (*Matthew* 16:19).

729   **mortal**   deadly.

731-4   Like Beëlzebub (I 143-52), Sin realizes that God must have preserved Satan for some purpose, which she believes to be the satisfaction of his derision (*laughs*, 191) and *wrath*. She is humanizing God too much, but it is true that Death and Satan will be the instruments of God's justice towards sinners.

732   **ordained his drudge**   designated his servant.

734   Jesus will destroy both Satan and Death at *the end* (*I Corinthians* 15: 24-28).

735   **the Hellish pest/Forbore**   Death (again unnamed) did not strike.

736   **these**   these words.

738   **Thou interposest**   you interrupt and thrust between (himself and Death).

738-40   **my sudden ... intends**   my hand, forestalled from an immediate blow, waits before it shows you (*tell thee by deeds*) its purpose.

742   **first met**   Sin is so changed (now *double-formed* as a snake-woman) that Satan does not realize he has known her before.

Sin Tells her Story: Lines 746–814

The incestuous relationships which Sin now describes must be read allegorically (see Approaches pp.180-1), as a parable of the self-love and self-destruction of sinning, or we will feel too much sympathy for Sin. Satan's 'marriage' with Sin and the birth of Death creates a Hellish Trinity which parodies the Holy Trinity of Father, Son, and the Holy Spirit who comes from both. Do you find the story revolting, or tragic, or too abstract to be either? What does it reveal about the psychology of sin (for example, the presence of self-hatred as well as self-love)?

746   **portress**   female gate-keeper.

748   **deemed**   thought.

749-51   The *assembly* of rebellious angels (*seraphim*) is described V 743-907.

756-8   The goddess Athena sprang fully armed out of the head of Zeus; Eve will be made out of the side of Adam and resemble him and God (VIII 465-471, *Genesis* 2:21-22). What do such myths seem to be saying about women?

757   **shining heavenly fair**   probably meant of Satan, then Lucifer (bringer of light).

761   **Portentous**   ominous, unlucky (as she is).

763   **the most adverse, thee chiefly**   those most opposed to me, particularly yourself.

764-5   On this self-reflective mirror, see Approaches p.147, p.180. Eve (like Narcissus) also briefly falls in love with her own reflection (IV 465-6).

765   **enamoured, joy**   words suggesting lust.

768   **fields**   battles.

770-1   **rout/Through all th'empyrean**   disorderly flight through Heaven (the *empyrean* is the region of upper fire); see Approaches p.148 for the events alluded to here.

772   **pitch**   height.

775   **with charge to keep**   Like Eve, Sin is given a responsibility (*charge*) by God, from which she will be tempted by Satan; see Approaches p.182 for a detailed discussion of the key.

778   **long I sat not**   it was not long before. Scarcely two weeks have passed since the fall of Satan, so gestation is quick.

779   **excessive**   ready to give birth or increase.

780   **Prodigious**   unnatural, portentous.

780   **rueful throes**   penitential pains (perhaps allegorizing the remorse after sinning).

784-5   Her lower (*nether*) part was transformed by the birth of Death into a snake's. She thus mirrors what Satan will become (IX 86, X 531).

785   **inbred**   bred inside me.

787-9   The name of *Death* is given by a kind of echo, recalling the reflections in the myth of Narcissus, who was loved by Echo.

794   **Ingendering ... begot**   that rape made us the parents (of the Hell-hounds).

796-800   This process was described more fully in 656-9 above, though their hunger (which mirrors Death's) was not mentioned then. Spenser's snake-woman, Error, herself poisons and eats her canine brood.

798   **list**   wish. One of the most sympathetic aspects of Sin is that she suffers others' acts rather than acting herself (though she did win Satan, 762).

801   **conscious terrors**   living terrors, but also the terrors of conscience which are born from sinning.

802   **rest or intermission**   Hell denies rest (see headnote to 506-69 above).

803   **in opposition**   opposite but also opposed to me. The

discord between the monsters would seem characteristic of Hell, but in fact they will soon form the same *concord* (497) as the rebel angels.

805 **devour** Like the *repast* of the Hell-hounds, Death's devouring of Sin would be another kind of rape. The hunger of Death is traditional, and seems here to express his negative power, like a black hole (see 705 above).

806-9 As Sin is the cause of Death, in destroying her he would destroy himself (she would be his poison or *bane*). As at 775, she avoids naming God, preferring the neutral term *fate*.

812 **invulnerable** safely immortal; as she has already prophesied (734) Satan can die. This answers the question about their own immortality which the fallen angels constantly return to (for example, see 153-4); only God, *who reigns above* never suffers death, and the rebel angels, unlike Mankind, will never be redeemed.

813 **mortal dint** fatal blow.

Satan Persuades Sin to Open the Gates of Hell: Lines 815-89

This is probably the best example in I and II of the cunning and hypocrisy of Satan (the *subtle fiend*). The deception in his previous speeches had always involved some self-deception, but here we know his real feelings about Sin and Death (see 681-745 and find words in this passage to contrast with words like *execrable* and *detestable* which are used there). Once he has *learned* his *lore* (that Sin has power to let him out of Hell, and that she was bound to him before being charged to guard the gates), everything he says to her will serve his purpose of getting to Earth. How many lies and contradictions can you find in his speech? Sin's speech reveals her consciousness that she will be violating duty (*due, owe, office*) by opening the gates, and her vulnerability to his flattery and promises. In the structure of the whole poem, her act is the first step in the process of the human tragedy. For the symbolism of the key, see Approaches p.182.

815   **lore**   lesson.

817   **sire**   father.

818-19   **pledge/Of dalliance**   sign of our mutual love-making (an extraordinary way to refer to Death).

821   This statement (if true) would provoke Belial's scorn (204-6).

822   **to set free**   although this is not Satan's main purpose (which is to revenge himself on God), seducing Mankind will in fact release Sin into the world.

825   **pretences**   intentions, claims.

827-30   Several of the words here (such as *uncouth*, meaning unknown) are taken from Beëlzebub's similarly off-putting description of Satan's journey (404-7).

827   **sole, and one for all**   alone and selflessly; there is courage as well as arrogance in this, but it parodies the genuine sacrifice of Jesus' *one for all*; see headnote to 390-429 above.

829   **unfounded**   without foundation, bottomless.

831   **by concurring signs**   by signs which substantiate the prophesy; he is right about these new details (Earth's shape and position) though we are not told what the *signs* were.

833   **purlieus**   neighbourhood (a position Beëlzebub only hoped for at 394-5).

834-7   The jealous suggestion that Mankind was created to fill up the space left by the angels' expulsion (though in fact Satan himself claims to have known about Mankind before the war), requires him to explain why Mankind was not placed in Heaven: they might then have proved too numerous (*surcharged*) and strong and rebelled against God (compare with 367).

837-8   **Be this ... now designed**   If God is plotting either this or anything even more secret.

842   **buxom**   yielding; like Beëlzebub at 394-402 above, Satan is using the charms of Earth to sell his plan.

842   **embalmed**   perfumed, made balmy.

844   In *Paradise Lost* neither Man nor nature is subject to death before Eve and Adam ate the fruit *whose mortal taste/Brought death into the world* (I 2-3).

846   Death is often depicted as a grinning skeleton.

847   **maw**   stomach.

848   **good hour**   the hour when the fruit is eaten and God betrayed.

849   **bespake**   spoke to.

850-1   **due ... King**   Sin now names God in order to establish her mandate of duty (*duty*) and obedience to keep the key.

853   **adamantine**   see note to 436 above.

855   **Fearless ... might**   Not fearing to be outclassed by any living power.

856-7   Sin appears to have more justification for this claim than Eve will, though she too feels *thrust down* by God (IX 759; see Approaches p.180).

858   **Tartarus**   see note to 69.

859   **office**   duty, responsibility.

862-3   Sin is surrounded (*compassed round*) by the horrors and sounds of her children: Death and the Hell-hounds.

864-6   Are you touched by these lines, or do you feel they express only the lonely psychology of sin?

868   **The gods who live at ease**   Mankind; she has misunderstood 834-7.

869   **At thy right hand voluptuous**   This parodies Jesus' seat at the right hand of his Father, though Sin expects a sexual (*voluptuous*) dimension as well.

869   **beseems**   is appropriate for.

871-2   **fatal key/Sad instrument**   Sin's misuse of the key is the equivalent of Eve's eating of the forbidden fruit in its moral effect: each object is a tragic *instrument* for the release of Satan, Death, and herself into human history (see 725 and Approaches p.182).

873   **bestial train**   her snaky tail.

874   **huge portcullis high updrew**   drew up high the huge inner grating.

875-6   **Which but ... moved**   None of the powers in Hell apart from herself could have begun to move.

877   **wards**   the projections on the key (which had *warded* against escape).

878   For the gate's mixed construction, see 645-7 above.

878 **ease** This prominently-placed word not only suggests *release* but also the moral truth that it is easier to admit than to exclude evil (see 884).

883 **Erebus** the lowest part of Hades.

883–4 Only Jesus has power to shut the gates (*Revelation* 1:18: *I have the keys of Hades and of Death*).

885 **bannered host** army with banners marching in open formation (*loose array*), visualizing Jesus' words *Matthew 7:13-14: wide is the gate, and broad is the way, that leadeth to destruction, and many there be who go in that way. Because narrow is the gate, and hard is the way, that leadeth unto life, and few there be that find it.*

Satan Crosses Chaos: Lines 890–950

We now have a dramatic change of perspective, as we turn from watching Satan to seeing with his eyes the immensity of Chaos, which contrasts so strikingly with the enclosed and *vaulted* Hell. It also contrasts with the order of Heaven, and so must draw on Milton's personal experience of the turmoil of Civil War (see Approaches pp.138-9). Should we see this as another psychological landscape? If we do, we should not forget that Milton seems to take his source (Ovid's *Metamorphoses* I 5-20) pretty literally: his Chaos is the receptacle (*womb*, 911) from which God created the world; see Approaches p.148. The formlessness and disorder of Chaos shows its distance from God, and also, in a half-comic way, its wild freedom from his control (*Chance governs all* – including whether Satan gets to Earth or not). Satan's resourcefulness also makes him appear a second Ulysses crossing an ancient sea (*hoary deep*), see Approaches p.171. How does Milton convey the difficulty of the journey (discussed in Approaches p.155 on the rhythm)?

891 **hoary** ancient (suggesting whiteness, which is immediately contradicted, in this confusing landscape, by *dark*).

894–5 **Night, Chaos** Rulers of Chaos, whose rule is an absence of rule (*anarchy*) see note to 988 below. There is a similar paradox in *by confusion stand*.

898–902   Milton personifies the qualities of the four elements (hot/fire, cold/air, moist/water, dry/earth) as the leaders (*champions*) of four armies of atoms. These atoms are *armed* with different qualities (for example, *swift* atoms are seen as *light-armed*) which encourages them to form different sub-groups (*factions* or *clans*), such as those which existed in Cromwell's unstable Commonwealth (see Approaches pp.144–5).

899   **maistrie**   mastery.

903–6   *Barca* and *Cyrene* were cities in an area of north Africa, which the traveller Heylin said was *all over covered with a light sand, which the winds remove continually up and down, turning valleys into hills, and hills into valleys.* The atoms, like sand, weigh down the *lighter wings* of the winds, like armies enlisted (*levied*) to fight one another.

904   **torrid**   hot and dry.

906–7   **To whom ... moment**   as the *atoms* keep changing their qualities, the quality to which most subscribe rules for that moment.

907–9   **umpire, arbiter**   names which reflect the absence of control of both Chaos and Chance; indeed Chaos's bad decisions confuse (*embroil*) the war (*fray*).

911   According to the Roman poet Lucretius, Nature was created out of the atoms of Chaos and would eventually disintegrate into them again (Prince ed. of *P.L.*).

913   **pregnant causes**   the reasons which determine why matter takes different forms. What other words suggest that Chaos is like a pregnant woman?

919   **frith**   strait (again suggesting Chaos is a sea).

920   **pealed**   made to ring.

921–7   Epic similes comparing the noise of Chaos to that of a battering-ram used in war-time (when the Goddess of War, *Bellona*, is active) to end (*raise*) a siege; or to cause the falling of the Earth and sky from its fixed position by some terrible catastrophe, yet this is also seen as a *small thing* in comparison with Chaos.

925–7   This almost seems to anticipate the modern concept of 'entropy', a degeneration of the material out of which the

Earth is made, though Milton imagines it happening not over billions of years, but suddenly, like a civil uprising (*mutiny*).

927   **sail-broad vans**   wings as broad as sails (suggesting he is a boat, as in 636).

928   **surging smoke**   perhaps emerging from Hell-gate (see 899).

929   **spurns**   kick away from.

931   **Audacious**   daring, defiant.

933   **plumb**   straight; see Approaches p.155 on this line.

935-6   Satan's fall is arrested by the blast thrown out by a cloud inflamed (*instinct*) with fire and saltpetre (used in gunpowder and thought to cause lightning and thunder), and he is thrown upwards.

938-9   **that fury ... Syrtis**   the hot blast is arrested by a quick-sand (named after the *Syrtis* in north Africa) which quenches it.

940   **nigh foundered on he fares**   he continues, though nearly sinking.

941   **crude consistence**   raw material.

942   **behoves ... sail**   he needs both feet and wings (the tone is comic).

943   Epic simile comparing Satan's journey to that of another creature with both legs and wings, a gryphon (lion with eagle's head) pursuing the one-eyed Scythian (*Armiaspian*) thieves of his gold. What do Satan and the gryphon have in common (apart from their versatile methods of travel)?

Satan's Encounter with the Rulers of Chaos: Lines 951–1009

Milton's ultimate source is Hesiod's *Theogomy*, which personified the attributes of nature as gods like Chaos, Erebus, and Night. Do you find Chaos and Night emerge here as real characters (see Approaches pp.180–1)? Again there is an element of comedy; Chaos, for example, looks *incomposed* and (as Broadbent pointed out) he does not finish his sentences. They are surrounded by attributes, taken from literature (Boccaccio and Spenser) rather than nature, who are even less clearly realized. Why, for example, is it Discord, and not Rumour, who has many tongues? But the probable purpose of the episode is not to explore the theology of Chaos, but to show again Satan's cunning in presenting his journey as one that will benefit these *anarchs*. Just as he tempted Sin to open the gates, so now he tempts Chaos (can you see where he tells lies?) to give him directions. Indeed, his promises come true in one way, for he will bring darkness and moral chaos to the Earth.

954	**loudest vehemence** an emphasis even louder than previous noises.
954	**plies** makes his way.
955	**Undaunted** This has the same force as *Unterrified* (708).
958-9	Satan needs to know the nearest place where the darkness of Chaos is illuminated by Heaven's light, as he knows Earth is close by Heaven.
959	**straight** straight away.
960	**pavilion** ceremonial tent.
961	**wasteful** desolate, laid waste.
962	**sable-vested** clad in black.
963	**consort** queen, but equal in power.
964-7	In Boccacio's *Genealogy of the Gods*, *Orrcus*, *Ades* (both personifications of Hades), *Rumour*, and *Discord* are all children of *Demogorgon*, the most ancient god (Hughes ed. of *P.L.*). See also Vergil's monsters in Appendix pp.196-7, discussed in Approaches p.172. Do you find this chant of strange names effective?
964	**the dreaded name** himself, in person. His name was used in magical invocations; Marlowe's Faustus uses it to invoke Mephistopheles.
970	**I come no spy** This statement contrasts with how Beëlzebub explained the journey in II 354.
977	**confine** border.
977-84	Satan begins his temptation by suggesting that God *won* Earth (*some other place*) from Chaos' territory. If Chaos agrees with this (absurd) interpretation, he should show

Satan the way there, so that Satan can recover it for Chaos.

980   **profound**   deep abyss (an adjective used as a noun).

982   **To your behoof**   to your benefit.

982   **lost**   lost to Chaos' kingdom.

982–5   **If I … journey**   If I, having expelled the intruder, restore Earth to its original chaos and your rule, I will have achieved the purpose of my present journey.

987   **revenge**   Satan's single-minded purpose contrasts with the wandering of his fellow-angels.

988   **anarch**   non-ruler.

989   **incomposed**   disturbed.

992   **Made head against**   threatened.

995–6   The repeated words in 995 and the repeated idea of confusion in 996 (to *confound* is to *throw into confusion*) express the disintegration as fall (*ruin*) is added to ruin, flight (*rout*) to flight.

996–8   The pursuit by the victorious angels is referred to at I 169–70 and 79 above.

999   **if all I can will serve**   if the most I can do will help at all (though the sentence is not finished).

1001–2   Their own civil wars are diminishing their own power (*sceptre*).

1002   Chaos here takes up Satan's suggestion (977–80) that God's creations are at his expense. Both Hell and the Universe (*heaven and earth*) were stolen from his kingdom (though again he does not finish his sentence).

1005   **golden chain**   an idea derived from Homer *Iliad* viii, 18–27, where Zeus says he can draw all things up to himself by a golden chain; this was allegorized as the *chain of being*; see Approaches p.146.

1007   **walk**   journey.

1008   **danger**   to whom?

1008   **speed**   succeed.

1009   **Havoc**   The order to *cry havoc* meant that *spoil* or booty could be seized. Chaos is looking forward to assimilating the ruins of the Universe (compare this with 921–7).

Satan Concludes his Journey:
Lines 1010–55

We find here more dramatic changes of perspective. First we follow Satan as he labours on towards Earth, then we look back and see Sin and Death building their bridge. Next with Satan's eyes we see *far off* the walls and light of Heaven, embodying all he has lost. Finally, we see our own Universe as if glimpsed from outer space – tiny, pure, and vulnerable – with Satan hurrying to spoil it. These shifts are not just shifts in space, but in time: Heaven was *once his native seat* in the past, Sin and Death will build their bridge *soon after when Man fell* in the future, but *he hies* to Earth in the present *cursed hour*. Our last sight of him is of his soul, full of revenge, malice, and danger, but also *accursed*, still impressive, and still pitiable.

1010   Satan's discourtesy shows his single-mindedness and hypocrisy.

1013   **pyramid** flame-shaped (suggesting *puri*, the Greek word for fire).

1016   **Environed** surrounded.

1016–20   Two epic similes of constricting journeys. The first compares Satan to Jason, who sailed in the *Argo* through the clashing rocks of the Syplegades at the eastern end of the Bosphorus (*justling rocks*), in order to get the golden fleece. The second relates him to Ulysses, who by steering to the left (*larboard*) successfully passed between the rock *Scylla* and the whirlpool *Charybdis* at the straits of Messina between Italy and Sicily (see 650 above).

1021–22   The repetition emphasizes Satan's difficulties.

1023   **soon after when Man fell** Milton here anticipates X 293–324 when, because Mankind has disobeyed God, Sin and Death are able to build a road from Hell for demons to ascend and humans to descend.

1024   **amain** without delay.

1026   **a broad and beaten way** a broad and much-used road, recalling the *broad … way that leadeth to destruction* (*Matthew* 7:13; see note to 885).

1029   **utmost orb** outer orbit of the Universe, the sphere of fixed stars, which Milton imagines as being surrounded by a protective shell.

1033 St. Augustine taught that one of the consequences of the fall of Adam is that human beings become much easier to tempt to do evil. The few who resist (for example, Noah) are guarded by *special grace* from God.

1037 Satan has reached the border between Nature (which has light and form) and Chaos (which is dark and formless). The light comes from Heaven, not the sun, which is orbiting the Earth far within the Universe; see picture on p.194.

1040-1 A pair of lines which parallel 1021-2, the repetition exposing the change.

1042 **dubious** uncertain, faint (like *glimmering* 1037).

1043-4 The image of the *weather-beaten vessel* recalls other metaphors of Satan as a ship crossing the sea of Chaos (for example, in 636 and 927), but may also be a poignant contrast with the song *Never weather-beaten sail* where the boat is an image of the soul finding port in Heaven. The *shrouds* (sails) also suggest a parallel with death.

1945 **emptier waste** less chaotic space (though not yet true *air*).

1046 **Weighs** hovers.

1048 **undetermined square or round** Since authorities differed on the shape of Heaven (Plato has it round, so that the Earth mirrors it; *Revelation* 21:16 has it *foursquare*), Milton leaves the question open by saying it was too *wide* to tell.

1049-50 See the description of Heaven from *Revelation* 21 on p.144.

1053 Compared to Heaven, the Universe looks as small as a star seen beside the moon.

1054 **fraught** laden (still like a ship).

1055 **hies** goes.

Approaches

Introduction

You may be wondering why you have to tackle this text. It may seem too difficult, too religious, and too far from your own concerns. To insist that it is the most wonderful literary text after Shakespeare is unlikely to convince you; tastes differ. To assert that Christianity is a central part of our culture and worth understanding is also something you might dispute. But after you have worked through the poem I hope you will no longer say that it is irrelevant or detached from your own most personal concerns. It is a poem which tackles the central problems of our lives: why evil exists, how essentially it differs from goodness, and whether we are free to choose between them. These problems are raised in terms of a fantasy which is at once realistic and universal. The story of Satan, in these two books, is about authority and revolt, heroism and deceit, and it is conveyed in a narrative style of such passionate electric energy that you will be unable to resist its power.

Milton's Life and the Political Context of the Poem

Early Life and Writings

Milton the poet (1608-74) was the son of another John Milton, a scrivener (a combination of lawyer and money-lender), who was not only financially very successful, but was also a talented musician and composer. He sent his son John to St. Paul's School, where he learned to write in both Latin and Greek, and to Christ's College Cambridge (1625-32), where he came fourth in the University for his BA and then stayed on to study further and to take his MA. His father expected him to become a clergyman, as he was a most fervent Christian, but his ideas were too independent and anti-royalist for the Church under Charles I (see next section). So, in 1632, he simply came home to Horton in Buckinghamshire to prepare himself to become a poet, learning French, Italian, and Hebrew as well as reading even more deeply in Classical Literature, all of which he was to use in *Paradise Lost*. He stayed there until he was nearly 30, and then he travelled to Italy, where he was already famous for his Latin and Italian poetry. However, he became so concerned about the increasing political and religious turmoil in England that he returned the following year, and in 1641 decided to put aside his chosen vocation and become a kind of free-lance commentator on events, in the hope that his stream of pamphlets would actually change government policy. His first volume of poems did, however, get published in January 1646 (title page says 1645), the year before the death of the father who had supported him so faithfully.

One of the central issues in *Paradise Lost* is the nature of freedom, and it is freedom that Milton defended all his public life. His first pamphlets were aimed at the Church, first to free it from the tyranny of bishops, and then, more personally, to urge it to permit freer divorce. For the first three years of his first marriage (1642–5) he was separated from his wife, and during this period he published a series of *Divorce Tracts*, which argued that one should be able to free oneself from an unworthy or incompatible partner. These were received unfavourably and he was nicknamed 'Milton the Divorcer'. In another tract he wrote in the same period, the *Areopagitica* (1644), he defends the freedom of the press. Here he argues that the reader should not be over-protected, but be exposed to both good and evil in what he reads. He makes a vivid comparison with the fruit of the Tree of Knowledge forbidden to Man in the Garden of Eden:

> It was from out the rinde of one apple tasted, that the knowledge of good and evil, as two twins cleaving together leapt forth into the World. And perhaps this is that doom which Adam fell into, of knowing good ... by evil.
>
> (*Selected Prose*, ed. D. Patrides, p.213)

(**Paraphrase:** When Adam and Eve ate the apple, good and evil, like Siamese twins, leapt into the world together: perhaps their punishment was that thereafter Man knew good by knowing it was not evil.)

In *Paradise Lost*, written more than 20 years later, Milton is still defending the right of every reasonable creature to have freedom of choice, even if, like Satan or Adam, he chooses to do evil.

Activity

Discuss the question Milton raises here: should we make ourselves aware of evil so that we can learn to prefer good? In your view does it do any harm to be exposed to books and films which delight in violence? Should one protect children's innocence as long as possible?

Discussion

In practice we cannot help being exposed to evils such as violence; the world itself is full of images of evil and destructive things as well as good ones, and both books and television reflect this. This is a problem only if you feel we are too weak to resist the allure of wickedness. One answer to the old problem *Why does a good God allow the world to be so full of evil?* might be that it is precisely to test our strength as individuals that God gives us choices between good and bad (see I 366, where Milton calls this *God's high sufferance for the trial of Man*). Without that choice we would not be free moral beings. In Book III of *Paradise Lost* God himself explains that he must give all his rational creatures (angels, men, and women) the freedom to choose between good and evil, because:

> Not free, what proof could they have given
> Of true allegiance, constant faith or love?...
> I formed them free, and free they must remain
> Till they enthrall themselves.   (III 97–125)

(**Paraphrase**: If they had not been free, they would not have been able to prove their faithfulness to me (and to goodness). I made them free, and they will remain so until they enslave themselves to sin.)

One can subscribe to this idea of morality as a choice even if one does not believe in the existence of God.

The Revolution

Paradise Lost is in one sense a political poem. It opens with Satan and his army recovering from a civil war in heaven which supposedly preceded the creation of the world. Book II is partly devoted to a parliamentary debate in which the issue of whether to continue the war against the royalty of God is debated. It is no coincidence that this was the period of England's worst Civil War (1642-9), in which the issue of freedom took centre stage in everyone's life. Milton took the side of the 'Roundheads', who fought for the subjects' freedom to rule themselves, against the 'Cavaliers' or Royalist party. The Roundheads' brilliant general, Oliver Cromwell, eventually defeated the Royalists and executed King Charles I in 1649. This was an act which Milton defended but which appalled many English people, even those who supported the new Commonwealth. However, we can see from these words from the triumphant Parliament's *Act for the Abolishing the Kingly Office* (17 March 1649) that it felt the king had become a tyrant and must be removed:

> It has been found by experience that [to place] the office of a king ... in any single person, is unnecessary, burdensome and dangerous to the liberty, safety, and public interest of the people, and that for the most part use has been made of the regal power and prerogative to oppress and impoverish and enslave the subject.
>
> (quoted in D.Wootton, *Divine Right and Democracy*, p.316.)

There is no space here to discuss why Charles I was thought to 'impoverish and enslave' his subjects; the charge was based principally on the fact that he ruled, and taxed, his subjects without calling a Parliament for an '11-years tyranny' (1629-40). The essential point for us is that Milton believed that in ridding itself both of this particular tyrant and kingship in general, England was recovering its original freedom. His tract *Of the Tenure of Kings and Magistrates*, written during Charles' trial, explains that to abolish kingship is to return to the original freedom of Adam and the equality of all people:

> all men naturally were born free, being the image and resemblance of God himself, and were by privilege above all the creatures, born to command and not to obey: and they lived so. Till from the root of *Adam's* transgression, falling among themselves to do wrong and violence ... they saw it needful to ordain some authority that might restrain by force and punishment what was violated against peace and common right.
>
> (*Selected Prose*, ed. D. Patrides, p. 255)

The central scene of *Paradise Lost* shows Satan tempting Adam and Eve to lose this original freedom by serving him rather than God.

Activity

Both Satan and Beëlzebub constantly claim that God is a tyrant who, in the words applied to Charles I in the quotation above, wants to *impoverish and enslave the subject*. But is God really like Charles I? Look at Satan's speech about Hell (I 241–70), and particularly at the way he speaks of God. Is it true that only *force* has made God supreme, and do you think that it is really *better to reign in Hell than serve in Heaven*?

Discussion

Let us imagine for a moment that this is not Satan speaking about God, but Oliver Cromwell speaking about Charles I in the unlikely event that Charles had won the Civil War. Phrases like *he/Who now is sovereign* (I 245–6) and *Whom thunder hath made greater* (I 258) then seem quite appropriate; they suggest that the tyrant-king (God) has only won a temporary victory by out-gunning the revolutionary army. (Satan's first speech, I 84–124, was full of such claims; the *potent Victor in his rage* was said to still hold *the tyranny of heaven*.) It would also be appropriate for a revolutionary leader to scornfully refuse to return to the *happy fields* (249) of the tyrant's kingdom and serve (263) in his court. It is far nobler to set up a government-in-exile and continue the revolutionary struggle. However, service to a king is not the same as service to God, which Milton believed to be the only route to personal happiness and freedom (see pp.146–7). Milton has used his revolutionary ideas to give Satan a good case, but we should not accept his view of God.

Milton in and out of Government

The publication of *Of the Tenure of Kings and Magistrates*, brought Milton to the attention of the Commonwealth leaders (the Council of State headed by Cromwell), who in March 1649 made Milton the Secretary for Foreign Tongues, with the responsibility of explaining and justifying their actions both at home and abroad; he was after all a superb linguist. Until 1655 Milton worked tirelessly to support the Commonwealth, publishing (among many other tracts) two *Defences of the English People* (in 1651 and 1654), which explained what the Commonwealth was trying to achieve. But privately he, like most of the

English people, was becoming increasingly dissatisfied with it. Instead of giving people greater freedom, Cromwell's authority as a military dictator actually curtailed their freedom. Cromwell refused to recognize the decisions of Parliament when he did not agree with them, delayed holding another general election until 1656, and then banned about 100 new Members from attending the new Parliament. There seemed no way of restraining him and his Council of State from arbitrary rule, and from 1658 Milton, who was now blind, increasingly spent time on *Paradise Lost* rather than defending a regime in which he could no longer believe, and a ruler who had become as bad a tyrant as the king had been. Instead he put Cromwell into his poem; Satan has much in common with this inspiring and gifted leader who was unable to avoid becoming a tyrant, and seems to provoke Milton's admiration as well as his disillusion. The poet William Blake, writing in 1790 with the success of another revolution (the French one) filling him with hope, even asserted that Milton was on Satan's side:

The reason Milton wrote in fetters when he wrote of Angels & God, and at liberty when of Devils & Hell, is because he was a true Poet, and of the Devils party without knowing it.
(*Marriage of Heaven and Hell*, Plate 5).

Cromwell's increase in power weakened the Commonwealth itself, and when he died in 1658 it fell apart, and the movement to recall Charles' son Charles II from exile in France became irresistible; the monarchy was restored in 1660. Milton was one of the very few who stuck to their republican principles and did not rejoice at home, or rush to cheer Charles on his ride to London, where the fountains ran with wine. Instead he published *A Ready and Easy Way to Establish a Free Commonwealth*, an act of courageous defiance which earned him a short stay in prison. His blindness (which was widely believed to be a punishment sent by God to one who had defended the execution of Charles I) probably saved his life, and he was allowed to retire quietly, marrying again (this time happily) in 1663. He occupied his time in writing poetry, often considering in it the thoughts and experiences which had preoccupied him during the most politically active period of his life. It took him seven years to complete his masterpiece, *Paradise Lost*, which was published in ten books in the first edition of 1667 (the basis for this text). A second edition in 12 books appeared in 1671, three years before his death; his payment for both was only £15. His other mature works include *Samson Agonistes*, in which he considers how one can achieve both virtue and success in spite of blindness, and *Paradise Regained*, a 'brief epic' in four books which shows Christ refuting Satan in the wilderness and so restoring Man to Heaven. These works record how triumph can be seized out of personal disaster – a triumph which Milton's life itself reflects.

Activity

In Book II the fallen angels debate what to do. Look at Mammon's picture of the life they would live in Heaven if they asked God for pardon (II 237–49), and compare it with these lines from *Samson Agonistes* (published 1671), in which Milton clearly attacks the English nation for restoring the monarchy:

> But what more oft in nations grown corrupt,
> And by their vices brought to servitude,
> Than to love bondage more than liberty,
> Bondage with ease than strenuous liberty ... (268–71)

Do you think Mammon's description might reflect Milton's hostility to the Restoration of Charles II ?

Discussion

In the passage from *Paradise Lost* Mammon reminds the angels of God's power to pardon the former rebels in words (*publish grace*) which suggest the Act of Indemnity which Charles II passed on being restored to the throne in 1660, 'pardoning all those who had taken part in the rebellion or the subsequent governments, except some 50 named individuals'; this 'reached a degree of clemency unusual in that cruel age' (*The Oxford History of England: 1660-1714*, p.4; see Further Reading p.186). Satan himself rejects the possibility of profiting by any *act of grace* in I 111 and in IV 94 (quoted below p.177), rather like Milton himself who preferred to go to prison than welcome Charles II. Mammon goes on to offer the angels a life of *hard liberty* in Hell, which seems very close to the *strenuous liberty* in Samson's speech. Both terms describe the difficult task of running one's own affairs, as in a Commonwealth, instead of accepting *bondage* under a king. Milton then would be in considerable sympathy with Mammon's point of view, were Mammon to be talking about Charles II. But Mammon is talking about God, who would never impose such bondage. As C.S. Lewis argues in *A Preface to Paradise Lost* (see Further Reading p.187), repentance is the only door that leads back to Heaven, and it is Satan, not God, who is shutting it, and so binding his fellow-angels in Hell. Just as Cromwell banned so many elected members from Parliament in 1656 because he was afraid they might undermine the revolution (and it was these members who eventually recalled Charles II), so Satan refuses to accept the majority decision reached in II 291–2, in favour of *peace*. Throughout the poem we see Satan robbing both his followers and Adam and Eve of their freedom in order to feed his own ambitious desires. Is Satan a true revolutionary, as Milton was, or a tyrant disguised?

The Religious Ideas in the Poem

Milton's Church

The desire for religious freedom was as much a part of the Revolution as the desire for political freedom. The Protestant Church in England (the Anglicans) had started as a kind of freedom movement, and many rejoiced when Henry the Eighth liberated England from the Pope by an Act of Supremacy in 1534 and made it Protestant. One difference that this made was that ordinary people were encouraged to read the Bible for themselves in translation; later, copies of James I's *Authorized Version* of 1611 could be found in every church. (This is the translation used in the Appendix.) In every way the Roman Catholic distinction between clergy and non-clergy was eroded: much of the wealth of the Church had been stripped away by Henry when he 'dissolved' the monasteries, the new clergy were allowed to marry, they conducted services in English, and they expected their parishioners to aspire to a much more exacting standard of virtue than had been the case when the priest would absolve people from their sins by the sacrament of penance. Even the look of the churches changed. The Catholic churches had tried to imitate the splendours of Heaven, but the Protestants preferred plainness and simplicity. The decorated statues to saints were removed, the stained glass was knocked out, and the altar was brought much closer to the people.

Activity

It has been said that Milton associates some of the pomp and extravagant trappings of the Catholic Church with Pandæmonium, Satan's parliament-house. Look closely at the description of Pandæmonium (I 713–30) and Satan's enthronement (II 1–10) and see how many words suggest wealth and display.

Discussion

Pandæmonium is surmounted by a *golden architrave* (I 715), ornamented with *bossy sculptures* (716) and has a golden roof; Satan's throne is *high* (II 1) and covered with jewels. It may be that Milton had in mind the Classical architecture and lavish decoration he had seen at St. Peter's Cathedral in Rome, where the Pope was enthroned, though Pandæmonium fits just as well in the poem as an entirely pagan temple, in which the pagan gods would feel at home (see picture p.191). But does its magnificence merely feed the angels' (and in particular Satan's) sense of self-importance? Could it not be that the fallen angels are merely trying to re-create the beauty of the Heaven they have lost, which is described in *Revelation* 21 in similar terms:

> [And the angel] showed me that great city, the holy Jerusalem, descending out of Heaven from God ... And the city lieth foursquare ... And the foundations of the city were *garnished with all manner of precious stones* ... And the twelve gates were twelve pearls ... *and the streets of the city were pure gold* ... And the city had no need of the sun, neither of the moon, to shine in it; for the glory of God did light it, and *the Lamb is the lamp of it*   (10–23).

I have italicized some of the points of correspondence and contrast between this city and Pandæmonium (see also note to I 728).

By the Seventeenth century, however, the young Protestant Church of England was itself beginning to restrict individual faith. Its beliefs and practices were not accepted by everyone; the oddities of Milton's personal religion (see next section) were characteristic of an age when some Christians were developing numerous *Independent* sects (such as the Ranters, Quakers, and Presbyterians), while others were trying to restore Catholicism. Both groups had their day. Seventeenth-century

Protestants had not forgotten that between 1553 and 1558 Queen Mary had attempted to restore the Catholic faith, by burning nearly 300 people. This was one of the reasons why Milton and many of his contemporaries disliked the Catholic faith, and why Charles I's sympathy towards it counted against him. The Roundheads who executed Charles were not just Protestant, they included a high proportion of Independents. They began to reorganize the Church of England, and to impose a rigorously puritan way of life on the people, encouraging high moral standards, plain living, hard work, and independence. In 1655 local 'major generals' were employed to see that people were attending Church regularly, and not going to parties or horse-races, or to the theatres, supposedly closed since 1342. Though Milton could be called both a puritan and an Independent, he argued strongly for religious toleration. However, the Commonwealth continued to enforce its own views, and this paved the way for the restoration not only of monarchy, but of the Church of England. One of Charles II's first Acts was to reopen the theatres. He tried also to restrict the Independents, imprisoning men like John Bunyan the Baptist, but he could not put the clock back any more than Mary had done, and from 1672 religious toleration became part of royal policy.

Activity

Go back to the speech by Mammon used in the Activity on p.142 and compare II 249–62 with the list of puritan values just outlined. Do any of the words he uses suggest he is offering a puritan way of life, and if so, why does he do so?

Discussion

Mammon seems to be trying to make life in Hell appear nobler and more dignified than the unchallenging and dependent life under the *easy yoke* (meaning harness, II 256) of Heaven (compare Satan's similar rejection of it I 263, discussed above p.142). He suggests the fallen angels will practise the virtues of self-sufficiency and independence, seeking *Our own good from ourselves* (253), and making *useful* things out of the *hurtful* materials of Hell (259). Their lives will be austere and hard-working, involving *labour and endurance* (262). As Mammon is the most materialistic of the fallen angels, we should take this with a pinch of salt. What he is really offering them, the *gems and gold* and the *Magnificence* of 271–3, hardly embody puritan values. It is typical of the leaders of the fallen angels that they call things by the names of their exact opposite. It is not until we meet Adam and Eve in Book IX that we can see an ideal way of life, that is comfortable and beautiful but also natural and simple.

Milton's Ideas on the Nature of Good and Evil

On the central issue of the nature of good and evil, of freedom, and of man's relation to God in general, Milton was perfectly orthodox. He derived many of his ideas from two of the principal founders of Christian theology, Protestant as well as Catholic: St. Paul (who wrote the *Epistles* in the New Testament) and St. Augustine (who lived in the Fourth century). St. Augustine had insisted that though goodness was a living reality, embodied in God, evil was not a power in itself, but a kind of negative impulse, an act of the will in preferring itself to God. To be happy as well as good, all creatures should accept their place in the hierarchy known as the 'chain of being', which looks like this:

God

Angels

Man

Woman

Animals

Plants

Minerals and other inanimate objects

Elements

All creatures should strive upwards towards God, and develop their potential by loving him (or loving goodness) as he loves them; hence the chain of being is sometimes called the 'chain of love'. Evil creatures, however, choose to move downwards, away from God and true being. Belial and Mammon, for example, want to avoid pain in Hell by becoming more like Hell, and so degenerating from their original being. We see this process beginning to happen to the other angels while they are waiting for Satan to complete his journey to Earth (II 506–628); they seem without real purpose, restless, and wandering. When Satan tried to depose God, he appeared to be trying to ascend upwards, but in reality he was replacing love of God by love of himself, and so instead of moving upwards, began to circle around his own desires and to spiral downwards away from God. (The same thing will happen to Adam and Eve when they try to become gods by eating the forbidden fruit, but in fact lose their immortality because they have replaced God's law by their own pride.) This self-reflective quality in evil is captured by Milton in the allegory of Sin: her marriages and births are all self-reflective, incestuous, unproductive, and degenerative (see p.180 below). Satan himself degenerates under our very eyes. The virtues which make him scarcely *less than Archangel ruined* at the beginning of Book I, begin to be corrupted by his own deceit; far from remaining *unchanged*, he is a flattering opportunist by the end of Book II, and by Book X seems small, spiteful, and snake-like.

Activity

A modern figure who is often thought to embody evil is Adolf Hitler. Compare Satan's speech to the assembled fallen angels (I 622–62) with the part of the speech made by Hitler in 1932 which is reproduced in the Appendix (p.200).

Discussion

In this speech, made during the great economic depression, Hitler blames the Germans themselves for the situation, saying they bear *a full measure of responsibility for our collapse,* and he implies that they will only recover if they vote for Hitler himself. Satan does not go so far as to blame his fellow-angels for their defeat, but he does excuse himself from blame (I 626–30, 635–7), and he too has a clear plan for recovery, *to work in close design, by fraud or guile* (I 646). Both see recovery as an ascent (Hitler's *road which leads upwards,* Satan's promise they will *re-ascend ... and re-possess their native seat,* 633), achieved by continuing warfare, not by reconciliation and peace. The results of such warfare will be self-glorification, not the achievement of some abstract good like the service of God or the establishment of peace and justice. Both therefore place themselves, and not God, at the top of the ascent, and try to infect their hearers with their own egotism. Both disguise their own inner degeneration by putting forward what seems to be an ordered plan, though it is in fact a plan which will spread further degeneration.

Milton's Ideas on Heaven, Hell, Angels, and Chaos

Milton's ideas about the natural and supernatural Universe were not as orthodox as his ideas on good and evil. Some even suggest the beliefs of the Ranters (an Independent sect mentioned p.144; see Hill *The World Turned Upside-down* in Further Reading p.186). The action of Books I and II does not take place within the Universe, but outside it. From reading the whole poem it is clear that the Universe is only a small part of an infinite and eternal space, of which the upper part is Heaven, which has limits, and the lower part Chaos, which has no limit. At a great distance below Heaven is placed Hell, which is walled and gated, but also seems to have no limit. God made all these parts out of himself, so none is intrinsically evil. First God made Heaven and the angels, then Chaos, and then Hell. The angels were divided into nine divisions, each under a different *archangel*; the leading archangel was called Lucifer, *bearer of light*. However, God then 'begot' Christ, and placed him next in power after himself. Lucifer took exception to being placed below Christ, and persuaded his own division of angels to rebel. There followed a great war in Heaven which was only ended when Christ himself mounted a chariot and drove the rebelling angels out of Heaven with his *ten-thousand thunders* (VI 836). They fell to the Hell God had prepared for them, and changed both their shape and their names (Lucifer becoming Satan). After (but not because) of this loss, God sent Christ to make the Universe out of the ingredients of Chaos (rather than out of nothingness, as in *Genesis*). Christ did this by stilling part of the sea of ingredients he found there, and ordering them into an Earth orbited by seven planets and three higher circles which included all the stars. He encased this revolving universe in a protective shell and hung it by a golden chain from the left side of Heaven (see II 1006). Finally, Christ made Man and Woman and placed them in the Garden of Eden near the River Tigris. The distance from Heaven to Hell as we learn in I 73-4, is three times the distance from the centre of the Earth to this outermost star-filled shell. But around and beyond the bounds of these finite places is the infinite abyss of Chaos (see sketch on p.194).

We should read this cosmology not as science but as a poetic myth, a model rather than a literal description of the truth (see p.168 below), particularly as it expresses neither the 'truth' of the Bible nor of contemporary science. Milton had visited Galileo (see note to I 287-91) and used his telescope to see into the real Universe, and indeed his description of the vast but not empty Chaos has some of the characteristics of outer space as we understand it. Yet his universe is therefore full of features which make poetic rather than scientific sense. For example, because he sees boundlessness as an aspect of formlessness, and opposed to the order and limit of Heaven, the number of fallen angels seems to grow during Book I, till by I 760 even their representatives are numbered in thousands. The implications of Milton's (genuine) belief that everything was created out of God are even more problematic. If the ingredients out of which Hell is made are no different from those of Heaven (I 670-85), how can it have been *Created evil, for evil only good* (II 623)? The fallen angels are themselves made from *empyreal substance* (I 117), that is to say, from the pure fire out of which Heaven itself is made, and they enjoy physical advantages which, particularly in Satan's case, help him to cross Chaos and deceive Adam. But if they were made out of God, how can they have been so disobedient to him? Here the science conveys the moral truth that it is the mind, and not matter, which can choose evil. God makes what is good; it is Satan and the angels who essentially create Hell by choosing themselves rather than God, and then continue the process of degeneration by wishing to become more like the Hell they have made.

Activity

Make a list of the attributes you would give to angels and fallen angels, and then compare it with I 116–7, 146–7, 225, and 423–31.

Discussion

Milton's fallen angels are much more like traditional angels than the small and monstrous devils shown for example in the Illustration (see p.191). Blake painted Milton's fallen angels like Greek gods, which is supported by the description of them as a super-human Greek army led by an *archangel ruined* (I 531–97), or by the description of Satan flying (I 225, II 631–5 – try painting this yourself). In general, the angels seem to glory in the strength and size of their 'natural' form (I 793), yet they also use the power inherent in their *empyreal substance* to change costume, shape, size, even sex (I 424–31). Although the fallen angels use this *essence pure* to fulfil *works of ... enmity* (I 431), such as Satan's deadly use of disguise in the Garden of Eden, the unfallen angels use it for *works of love*, and in Book VIII Raphael tells us about their power to make love:

> Easier than air with air, if spirits embrace,
> Total they mix, union of pure with pure
> Desiring;   VIII 626–8

It is the will, and not the nature of God's creatures, which allows them to do evil.

It remains a problem for most readers, however, that so many of God's supposedly pure angels did choose to follow Satan and rebel against God. This part of the story is not even taken directly from the Bible. There are, it is true, isolated passages referring to a war in Heaven, to Satan the tempter, to the fall of Lucifer, and even to the existence of Hell (see Appendix p.195), but nothing to justify the elaborate story that Milton tells. Milton did not, however, invent it. It was between the First and Fourth centuries AD that the early theologians or 'Church Fathers' developed the story of the rebellion of the angels, placed it at the beginning of the world (when God *divided the light from the darkness*: Genesis 1:4), and used it to explain why Man ate the fruit of the tree of knowledge. If Satan was the tempter, disguised as the serpent who actually does the tempting in the Bible, that would explain why Adam, then seen as the perfect and innocent natural man, could disobey God's law so easily, answering the question Milton puts at I 27–32. Adam's sin can be seen as the cause of all sin, all woe, and all pain, spoiling God's originally perfect world. Its punishment was death, or, since souls are immortal, the sending of Adam and Eve and all their descendants into Hell. Christ 'redeemed' Mankind by paying for the Original Sin of eating the apple with his own death on the cross. On Good Friday he was believed to have entered Hell and to have overcome both Death and Satan (this moment is referred to at II 721), and then to have led all the descendants of Adam up to Heaven. Since then no man would die and go automatically to Hell as Adam had done, but would be judged, and have the chance of entering either Hell or Heaven. It is in this way that *one greater Man*, Christ, has restored us to *the blissful seat* (I

4). The invention of the story of the fall of Satan therefore allowed theologians to explain not only the fall of Man but the Redemption of Christ, and it made something other than God or Man responsible for the (otherwise incomprehensible) presence of evil in God's good creation.

Activity

Milton claims he will *justify the ways of God to men* (I 26). (This means justifying God's treatment of Man, not of Satan, whom we expect to be punished.) Use I 211–18 to work out how he begins to do this in Books I and II.

Discussion

Making God the source of all things makes him ultimately responsible for everything which happens, in spite of the claim that his creatures have freedom; it implies that he wants human beings to suffer. One justification for this was outlined in the section on *Areopagitica* (pp.137–8) where it was argued that God actually wanted evil to exist in order to allow moral choice. This might be seen here as the *high permission of all-judging Heaven* (I 212). Milton goes on to offer another explanation for God permitting Satan to be *at large* (free). Although if Mankind had been *found obedient* they would have eventually ascended to Heaven, their disobedience meant that God had to send Christ to Earth to save them, and this was an even better manifestation of *Infinite goodness* (218). God showed him this *grace and mercy* (218) partly because he had been *seduced* (meaning tempted to disobedience, 219) by Satan, who lied to Eve about the effects of eating the fruit. As God explains in Book III, if Man had sinned at *his own suggestion*, as Satan (*the other*) did, he could not so easily have been forgiven:

> The first sort [angels] by their own suggestion fell
> Self-tempted, self-depraved: Man falls deceived
> By the other first: Man therefore shall find grace
> The other none. (III 129–32)

If you look at the passages in which Satan or Beëlzebub plot the overthrow of Mankind (I 650–9, II 344–78, 830–44, 979–87) you will see how vulnerable and innocent Mankind seems, the prey of Satan's revenge. But of course this raises the question again of why God made Man so weak and vulnerable to sin. To some extent then Milton's characterization of Satan justifies *the ways of God to men*. But ultimately Milton's task is impossible. It is a matter of faith whether we believe that God exists, and if he does, that he is good and cares for his creatures.

Charting the Themes

The thematic structure of *Paradise Lost* is based on the opposition between good and evil. The sentences are often constructed as 'antitheses', or pairs of opposites, and the fallen angels are characterized as negations of true virtue, desiring the opposite of good. It is worth making a list of such oppositions and adding examples to it as you come across them. You will then have a list of references on which to base discussion of such subjects as the religious structure of the poem, the moral deterioration of the characters, or the philosophical basis of the language. The following chart gives some of the oppositions, with one example for each. You could write in others.

Themes Chart		
Opposition	**One example**	**Your additional examples**
Heaven/Hell	I 255	
good/evil	I 216–8	
light/darkness	I 244–5	
ascent/descent	I 43, 45	
love/hate	II 248–9	
hope/despair	II 142–3	
virtue/vice	II 116	
truth/lies	I 126	
rest/restlessness	I 66	
purposiveness/ wandering	II 561	
true/false creativity	I 695–9	
service to God/spurious freedom in Hell	I 263	

Milton's Poetic Technique

Milton's poetry has certain characteristics which are peculiar to him, and learning to savour these will not only help you to enjoy the poem, but to answer any question concerning style and effect. These characteristics include, in summary: his musical use of rhythm and sound effects; his Latinate use of English in which the position of words in the line is crucial; his half-visual, half-abstract use of imagery and description; and his command of rhetoric, or the art of persuasive public speaking, which grows naturally from his political life. Understanding more why Milton writes as he does should help you to approach the delights and difficulties of the poem.

Reading Milton's Sensuous Music: Rhythm and Sound-effects

Milton was fascinated by music and by language. He liked to play his organ and sing every day, and one of his first important works was a masque (a short play with music and effects) undertaken in 1634 with the encouragement of the composer Lawes, who set the songs to music. It is usually called by the name of the villain, Comus, who is a prototype for Satan: an attractive, music-loving demon who tempts men to drink a wine that turns them to beasts:

> Rigor now is gone to bed
> And Advice, with scrupulous head, . . .
> What hath night to do with sleep?
> Night hath better sweets to prove,
> Venus now wakes, and wakens Love.
> Come, let us our rites begin
> 'Tis only daylight that makes Sin.

(Comus 107–26)

As sometimes in *Paradise Lost* one suspects that Milton too had a night-self, delighting in music, love, and licence, which emerges in his poetry when he puts Rigor (rigour), his day-self, to sleep. Comus' rhythmic emotional verse here is much more appealing than that of the good characters who speak in **blank verse** (unrhymed but rhythmically regular lines). One of the achievements of *Paradise Lost* is to make his blank verse as exciting and dynamic as Comus' music. The next two sections will show how he does this.

Rhythm

In his *Introduction* to the second edition of *Paradise Lost* (1674), Milton explains why he chose to write in blank verse rather than rhyme. As so often with Milton, his priority is to achieve greater freedom:

> This neglect of rhyme … is to be esteemed as an example set, the first in English, of ancient liberty recovered to heroic poem from the troublesome and modern bondage of rhyming.

He also explains how he will put that freedom under certain restraints: *apt number* (referring to variation in rhythmic effect to suit the sense); *fit quantity of syllables* (referring to the strict syllable count); and *the sense variously drawn out from one verse into another* (verse here meaning line, so that he is describing how his lines build up a long chain of meaning). The basic characteristics of Milton's poem are therefore a regular rhythm in unrhymed lines which are all of precisely the same length, and long sentences which carry the meaning through several lines.

The excitement of the poetry, like music one can dance to, comes from the beat. Every line of *Paradise Lost* is a **pentameter**, that is to say, it can be divided into five musical 'bars', known as feet. Each bar or foot consists of two syllables, of which the second is the stronger and more important (hence their name **iambs**). The skill of the poet is in arranging words which naturally fit this insistent rhythm. For example take the line:

```
 u   /   u   /   u   /    u   /    u  /
```
And swims or sinks, or wades, or creeps, or flies.   (II 950)

I have placed a *u* over the unstressed syllable, and / over the stressed one to indicate the effect, but you do not have to think about it: it will come from the natural stress of the words Milton has chosen (one would not normally accent *or*).

Activity

Read aloud Satan's rousing call to his stunned army (I 322–30), while your partner marks the unstressed and stressed syllables in pencil in the book. Feel the rhythm coursing through and carrying the long sentences along.

Because an alteration of stressed and unstressed syllables is natural to spoken English, it is perfectly possible for Milton, like Shakespeare, to write almost entirely in **iambic pentameters** without sounding forced or unnatural; Shakespeare, though more loosely, uses iambic pentameters for most of his lines without many people even noticing he is writing poetry. Milton's iambic pentameters are stricter than Shakespeare's, but occasionally he does vary the pattern by substituting another kind of foot for one of the iambs. For example, on the journey across Chaos, Satan first flutters his wings (*pennons*), and then he drops like a stone:

```
 /  u   u   /   u   /   /     /  u   /
Flutt'ring his pennons vain plumb down he drops          (II 933)
```

This line contains three true iambs (can you find them?) but it begins with a **trochee** or iamb in reverse (*/ u*) giving a quickly-moving pair of unstressed syllables, and it includes a **spondee** (two stressed syllables */ /*) to suggest Satan's heavy fall. Spondees are fairly rare because they slow down the rhythm, but they are very effective when they occur. See for example line 948 in the same passage, where Milton is again conveying how hard it is to get through the varied terrain (spondees in bold):

```
 u   /  u   /    /    /    /    /  u  /
O'er bog or steep, through strait, rough, dense, or rare   (II 948)
```

Now look at the first two syllables of the previous quotation: Milton has reversed the first foot (*flutt'ring*) to form a trochee (*/ u*) which has the result, in this particular line, of putting two unstressed syllables next to each other, like quick wing-beats. This first foot reversal is fairly common as it allows Milton to accentuate the first word in the line (for example, *Down had been falling*, 935). Variations like this depend for their effectiveness on the fact that generally he writes a very regular iambic pentameter. In the text I have therefore occasionally used accents to stress particular syllables so as to maintain Milton's insistent beat.

Activity

Scan (put in marks for rhythm) Belial's imagining of how each of the fallen angels might one day be chained on a separate rock (II 184–6). What is the effect of the rhythm here?

Discussion

Scanning is not an exact science, but one answer would be:

```
 /   u   u  /     u  / u / u     /
There to converse with everlasting groans,
 /  u  /  u   u /  u   /  u,  /
Unrespited, unpitied, unreprieved,
 /  u  u  /    u   /    /   u   u   /
Ages of hopeless end; this would be worse.
```

The natural stress of each word is used to build up a feeling of heavy, hopeless, endless torture, but each line has the right number of stressed and unstressed syllables; Milton has simply reversed the first foot of every line. The middle line stresses the *un* suggesting a negative, hopeless longing; the last line makes one linger on *Ages*, on *end* and on *this*; the first two suggest length of time, and *this* dramatically sums up the whole passage and refers back to Moloch's speech (*what can be worse* ... , II 85).

Sound effects

This passage about the journey across Chaos also contains examples of other aspects of Milton's music, particularly his use of repeated sounds. Repetition of the same sound in two different words always calls attention to itself, and can link words or even suggest the thing they describe (this is called **onomatopoeia**). Repetition of the same consonant in different words is called **alliteration**, and repetition of the same vowel-sound is called **assonance**. Both are used when Satan meets the *vast vacuity* of Chaos (II 932), where two words are linked by the repeated *v* (it is a *vacuity* because it is so *vast*), while the open vowels suggest the sense of terrifying distances. An even more onomatopoeic effect is achieved when he describes a puffing cloud:

> The strong **rebuff** of some **tumultuous** cloud.   (II 936)

Practically every line has some such effect; remember that this is poetry to be read aloud, with as much drama and variety as possible. It is not, however, always worth looking for a meaning within the sound, as some seem purely decorative, for example the exotic place-names which pour out like a musical fountain in the parade of the Gods, I 376–521.

Activity

How are alliteration and assonance used to convey meaning in the description of the fallen angels' applause (II 285–90)?

Discussion

The applause is muted, almost unconscious; the fallen angels welcome Mammon's shameful peace-proposal because they have been reminded by Belial of the terrifying storm of God's anger. Milton suggests this by comparing the applause to the *murmur* of the sea heard not during a storm, but *after the tempest* (290), as it echoes and booms in a cave (note the assonant *o* in *hollow rocks* and *hoarse cadence* 285, 287). This is contrasted with the loud *blustering winds* which had *roused the sea* the previous night (286–7: note the whistling sound of the alliterated *r* and *s*). The angels have had enough storms and even their applause is languid.

Understanding Milton's Latinate English

Milton uses English in a very peculiar way, which makes him difficult to understand until you get used to his style. Partly because he wanted his poem to feel Classical (see below p.167), he uses English as if it were Latin: he has a very wide vocabulary which often assumes you know the Latin word from which the English one has descended (these are explained in the Notes), he upsets the normal English word order in all sorts of ways, and the sentences themselves are very long and complex.

The biggest problem is generally the word order (which in normal English tells you the grammatical construction of the sentence). It is important to sort out what the word order would normally be, and although this is done for you in the Notes (particularly at the beginning) it is worth 'translating' every line into clear modern English until you feel able to understand it automatically. The problem can be illustrated by comparing the simple sentence *John liked the dog* with the sentence *The dog liked John*. It is because of the word order that you know that *John* is the subject of *like* in the first sentence (in other words, he does the liking), and that the *dog* is the object (in other words, he is liked). In the second sentence *The dog* is the subject, and *John* is the object. But Milton is quite ready to say *Him the Almighty power/Hurled headlong* instead of *The Almighty power hurled him headlong* (I 44-5). We have a clue as to who is being hurled because Milton says *him* and not *he*. Then again Milton likes to put subclauses (mini-sentences) in before he gets to the subject. For example, he tells us it was *Nine times the space that measures day and night* before he gives us the main clause *he ... lay vanquished* (50-2). Here again we have a clue to the subject, because Milton says *he* and not *him*. It is important not to miss such clues; Milton's sentences are always precisely grammatical once you have sorted them out. He also likes to move nouns and adjectives about, saying, for example, *A dungeon horrible* (I 61) rather than *a horrible dungeon* (these are known as inversions). The main poetic effects of changing the natural order of the sentences is to give the poem its precise, emphatic beat, and to highlight important words, placing them at the beginning or the end of lines. Noticing the position of words in the line is a key to analysing the poem stylistically.

Activity

Put II 981–6 into modern English prose, marking all the inversions you have turned round; is anything lost from the poetic effect?

Discussion

Although the preceding punctuation-mark is a semi-colon, often used by Milton instead of a full stop (see p.viii), these lines form a complete sentence which is linked to the preceding sentence by *Directed (if my course is directed by you it will ...)*. It could be expressed in modern prose: 'Your directing of my way (subject) will bring (main verb) you (indirect object) a large recompense (object), if I manage to reduce that lost region (*region lost* is an inversion) to its original darkness and your power, having expelled all invaders (*usurpation expelled* is an inversion).' Turning the inversions round means that Milton's emphasis on the verbs (*lost, expelled, reduced*) is lost. Moreover, its original complexity also suggests that Satan is being super-subtle. Some of his other complex sentences have the same over-clever and untrustworthy effect; can you find any?

Another problem with the sentences is their length. In order to work them out it helps to break them down into sub-sentences, and to see how they fit together like a jigsaw; see the next activity for an example of how this can be done. Again I have tried to resolve some of the ambiguities in the Notes. Watch out also for Milton's use of double negatives to cancel each other out. If the angels *nor ... not feel* their pains (I 335–6), it means they did feel them. As usual it is important not to miss a single clue to Milton's meaning.

Activity

Break down the first sentence of the poem I 1–16, into its component sub-sentences (clauses). Why do you think Milton opened his poem with such a convoluted first sentence?

Discussion

It may help your analysis if you understand a bit about the grammar here. The sentence begins with the **possessive** case: *Of Man's first disobedience* and only reaches the main subject and verb in line 6: *Sing heavenly Muse* (the *Muse* is the subject, and the verb is *sing*). All the other sub-sentences are attached either to *sing* (e.g. *of the fruit*) or *Muse* (e.g. *that on the secret top*), until you get to the semi-colon in line 10. The second part of the sentence has *I* as its subject and invoke as its main verb, and the sub-sentences are attached to *song*.

One of the reasons for opening the poem in this way is that it echoes the first sentence of Homer's *Iliad* (see p.167), which begins:

> Rage – Goddess, sing the rage of Peleus' son Achilles,
> murderous, doomed, that cost the Achaeans countless losses,
> hurling down to the house of Death so many sturdy souls ...

Both poets begin with the crucial subject of their poems: the human flaw which caused *all our woe* (I 3), though they differ about what that flaw is.

Imagery and Description

It may be helpful for appreciating *Paradise Lost* to know a little about the conditions under which it was written. When Milton began *Paradise Lost* in 1658, he had already been totally blind for six years. He dictated the poem to his two elder daughters, who were about 12 and 14 when he started it, and had learned to read to him not only in English but also in Hebrew, Latin, and Greek (which they did not understand). He would compose about 50 lines at a time, often at night or in the early morning, and would then ask to be 'milked' by dictating them. As Lois Potter says in *A Preface to Milton* (see Further Reading p.186), '*Paradise Lost* was, above all, a poem meant to be *heard*.' (p.32). Milton's eyesight was always poor, and it is tempting to think that this is why his images are often abstract and scholarly, and his descriptions sometimes dream-like and surreal. In the following lines from *Paradise Lost* Book III Milton considers his blindness, which seems to have begun as a 'mist'-like cataract, and explains the kind of poetry he is best suited to write:

> Thus with the year
> Seasons return, but not to me returns
> Day, or the sweet approach of even or morn,
> Or sight of vernal bloom, or summer's rose,
> Or flocks, or herds, or human face divine;
> But cloud in stead, and ever-during dark
> Surrounds me, from the cheerful ways of men
> Cut off, and for the book of knowledge fair
> Presented with a universal blank
> Of nature's works to me expunged and razed,
> And wisdom at one entrance quite shut out.
> So much the rather, thou celestial Light,
> Shine inward, and the mind through all her powers
> Irradiate, there plant eyes, all mist from thence
> Purge and disperse, that I may see and tell
> Of things invisible to mortal sight.   (III 40–55)

[*vernal* springtime; *ever-during* ever-enduring; *expunged and razed* rubbed out; *irradiate* shine throughout.]

You could say that the most striking characteristics of Milton's poetry here are the non-visual ones we have been considering already:

● the rhythmic build-up of phrases in lines 42–4, where the commas come increasingly quickly to increase the sense of longing.
● the musical effects like alliteration (*ever-during dark*, 45).
● the precise choice and placing of effective words, such as the shock of *dark* and *blank* at the ends of lines.

But also characteristic of his style are the half-formed images (of the spring flowers, or of his visual field as a piece of paper which has had all the pictures rubbed out). These images are half-abstract, half-visualized, always focusing on meaning. For example, the *sweet approach of even or morn* (42) is not precisely visualized, but it does convey his emotional loss in not in being able to *see* the passing of time. Such effects are often referred to as **transferred epithets**, where the adjective (*epithet*) tells you less about an object than about the person who is looking at it (for example, Satan looks at *regions of sorrow*).

Because his writing was already a mixture of the concrete and the abstract, Milton feels able to *turn inward* and describe *things invisible to mortal sight*. These include ideas and feelings, such as the principle of freedom, or the political ambitions of Satan. His writing therefore appeals to the mind, using lots of exciting verbal paradoxes and other linguistic surprises. For example, he uses **oxymorons** (two adjacent words suggesting contradictory ideas, see *darkness visible*, I 63), and **antitheses** (putting two opposite ideas against each other, often as a choice, see *Yours be th'advantage all, mine the revenge*, II 987). More of these techniques are explained under Persuasive Writing (see pp. 163–5). But his writing also appeals to the imagination, for he did not need eyes to create the supernatural beings which populate the poem, the fires of Hell, or the *Celestial Light* of Heaven. These descriptions may seem to you to be extremely vivid, even nightmarish, or they may seem only suggestive, allowing you to use your own imagination to flesh out the half-formed images which crowd in an intoxicating and often contradictory confusion.

Activity

Use the bullet-points and terminology of the preceding two paragraphs to analyse the effectiveness of Milton's first description of Hell (I 56–74) in arousing our horror.

Discussion

At first Milton's Hell seems fairly traditional, the poetry focusing on the horror of darkness and intense heat. For example the onomatopoeic alliterated *f* and the four strongly-stressed syllables in *As one great furnace flamed* (62) is slow and insistent. The prominent positioning of phrases like *No light* and *darkness visible* at the beginning and end of a line (63) help to emphasize the almost touchable darkness. But can we visualize such an effect? *Darkness visible* is a self-contradiction, an oxymoron, which alerts us to an abstract feature of Hell: its chaotic and self-contradictory nature. And as we follow Satan's gaze around, we experience the mental suffering more than the physical. The *transferred epithets* of *sights of woe* (64) and *Regions of sorrow* (65) suggest the fallen angels' sorrow, and the mention of *hope ... That comes to all* (66–7), which is an opposite or antithesis of *despair*, makes their despair seem all the more isolating. These are mental rather than visual effects, and they suggest that Hell is as much inside as outside Satan. The landscape arouses our horror by depriving Satan of all the positives which make life worth living.

Similar effects can be seen in the other descriptions of Hell reproduced in the Appendix. For example, Mephistopheles in *Dr Faustus* (Appendix pp.197–8) claims that Hell has no fixed place, *for where we are is hell*, and Garcin in *Huis Clos* (Appendix pp.198–9) knows that *One never sleeps*. But Sartre has to have a set without a bed, but with a bronze object which has somehow to look evil, to evoke the atmosphere. As a poet Milton can be more suggestive than a playwright, and he can also direct our feelings by charging his landscape with emotion.

Activity

Look at the passage in I 670–90 and find all the words which suggest a half-formed image of Hell as a body. What is the effect of this body imagery?

Discussion

Hell had been seen in the Middle Ages as a huge mouth, where the devils often eat, digest, and defecate sinners as part of their torture (see picture on p.192). Milton also likes to use the most degraded functions of the body in Hellish images and metaphors; Satan flies like a volcano farting *with stench and smoke* (I 237), and here a volcano *belched fire and smoke* and seems to be troubled with dandruff. Moreover, the body seems to be a female one, which the fallen angels actually seem to be raping (*ransacked the centre, rifled the bowels, digged out ribs*). Such images are disgustingly tactile (Milton had not lost his sense of touch); they express the degradation and perversion which runs through all the descriptions of Hell, where everything is monstrous, self-contradictory, and self-destructive:

Where all life dies, death lives, and nature breeds
Perverse, all monstrous, all prodigious things (II 624–5).

This self-contradiction is expressed most hideously in the female character Sin, whose body is continually entered and devoured by her own children (see p.180). The association of evil with female figures is of course a problem for the modern reader; in the Seventeenth century they were, unfortunately, more used to it. However, it must be partly because the female body is creative that Milton used it to suggest the perverse creation of evil and sin, which he believed were not made by God. This theme of false creativity runs right through the poem (see I 352, 501, II 766–7).

Debate and Speeches

Even schoolboys in Milton's day had *rhetoric* (the art of public speaking) on their curriculum, and students at Cambridge were expected to participate in formal academic debates which were marked. Milton excelled in this exercise, and used his debating experience in the polemical literature (tracts which argued for a particular course of government action) he produced in the 1640s and 50s (see pp.139-40). He developed his oral skill not just by reading the Classical orators (such as Cicero and Quintilian), but by listening to the live debates conducted at every level of society during these politically challenging years. At school he would have been taught to construct or analyse speeches by Classical subdivisions. A list of these, taken from the *Ad Herennium* attributed to Cicero, is given at the beginning of the Notes for Book II on pp.92-3, and an example of how to analyse a speech using them is given in the notes to I 622-69.

Persuasion in modern terminology

The purpose of a speech, as distinct from, for example, a discussion, is to persuade. The speeches in *Paradise Lost* are effective in the same way as the ordinary narrative; there is the same precise choice and positioning of words, the same sweep of the rhythm, and the same half-spoken images. But the speeches of the fallen angels often use a more heightened style, a style which is essentially *deceitful* in the way the ordinary narrative is not. They work by imposing the speaker's viewpoint on the audience. Consequently, one can analyse them as self-consciously persuasive. Modern advertising is also purposively persuasive and even deceitful, and Milton's angels could be said to use some of its methods:

packaging   calling things by false names, for example by referring to God as *Foe, Torturer, Adversary* etc., to prevent the angels from considering peace, and suggesting that the angels are heroes, or victims of fate.

imaginative constructions   or building up pictures of what a possible future might be like, for example, when Moloch (II 61–70) demonstrates how the fallen angels might renew the fight using Hell itself as a weapon.

appealing to powerful hidden feelings   such as fear, greed, or the desire for a quiet life, for example, when Belial *counselled ignoble ease* (II 227) and also terrifies his audience with a vision of increased pain (II 174–86).

use of sound-bites   to fix ideas in the audience's memory, often by appealing to their musical sense, for example, when Satan sneers at his fallen angels as *rolling in the flood* (I 324) (the *l*-sounds suggest the wallowing), and rouses them by the staccato, broken rhythm of *Awake, arise, or be for ever fallen* (I 330).

Activity

In II 393–402 Beëlzebub develops his proposal, introduced at 345, that the fallen angels should rob planet Earth from Mankind, and he wants them to adopt this, and not *peace* (292), as their policy. Imagine Beëlzebub is an estate agent trying to 'sell' Earth as a desirable residence to the fallen angels. How does he use the methods just listed?

Discussion

Beëlzebub has already packaged this plan as an *easier enterprise* (345) than fighting – just as an estate agent might say that one property was more 'affordable' than another. Here he tells them of the advantages of occupying Earth. It offers fine views (394), light (397–8), and (in a mouth-watering soundbite) *soft delicious air* (400). He appeals to their powerful hidden feelings by alluding to their present sufferings (*corrosive fires,* 401) and dangling the delusive hope that they might be able to move on from Earth to *re-enter* (397) the Heaven they secretly miss.

Persuasion in Classical terminology

It will be becoming clear that the terms we have been using overlap one another, and are very broad. You may prefer to use the more specific Classical terminology Milton would have recognized in order to particularize and clarify them. Unlike modern advertisers, or Milton's angels, orators were expected to be virtuous, and to appeal to the nobler parts of their audience, which was expressed in terms of their **ethos** or moral values (such as honour), their **logos**, or reason, and their **pathos** or passions. Milton knows that values, reason, and feelings can all be used as agents for corruption, as shown in the two preceding activities. Orators were also encouraged to use striking words in the most effective and emphatic order, and to ornament them with rhetorical figures of speech. These are of course to be found in the narrative sections of the poem as well (some were defined under Imagery and Description on pp.159-61), but in the speeches they have a particular didactic or persuasive purpose, which must always be understood to appreciate their effect. The following are a selection:

rhetorical questions   questions to which the answer is obvious and so not given, for example, *in this abject posture have ye sworn/T'adore the Conqueror* (I 322-3)

trope   an alteration of a word from its usual meaning, for example, Hell described as *this vast recess* (II 254)

amplification   saying the same thing several ways, for example, *O prince, O chief of many thronèd powers* (I 128)

anaphora   the parallel patterning of verbal structures, for example, *whom shall we send ... whom shall we find* (II 402-3)

chiasmus   a phrase which is then virtually repeated in reverse order, for example: *For happy though but ill, for ill not worst* (II 224).

Activity

Look at the quotations given as examples in the list above. Using your knowledge of their context, work out how each device makes the quotation more effective in persuading or manipulating the audience.

Discussion

Satan's scornful rhetorical question *'in this abject posture have ye sworn/To'adore the Conqueror* (I 322–3) makes the fallen angels see themselves degraded by their position; only by getting up can they really reply 'No!'. However, when Mammon calls Hell *a vast recess* (II 254) he is soothing their humiliation; altering the meaning of the word recess (alcove) to mean their dungeon, is a trope which acts as a euphemism (a mild rather than a blunt term). Beëlzebub's address to Satan as *O prince, O chief of many throned powers* (I 128), amplifies the flattering allusion to Satan's continued royalty. When he later asks the angels *whom shall we send ... whom shall we find* (II 402–3) the anaphora or parallel sentence-structure emphasizes the difficulty of finding the right person, and helps persuade the angels not to volunteer. Finally, when Belial describes *their present lot* by the chiasmus: *For happy though but ill, for ill not worst* (II 224), he is putting *ill* at the centre of the line and comparing it first with the happiness they have lost, and then with the suffering they could be enduring; this helps persuade them to stay as they are.

Activity

Look at the third section of Belial's speech (II 142–59) in which he attacks Moloch's suggestion that annihilation would be better than their present suffering. Use the modern and the Classical terminology just discussed to analyse how he tries to persuade the audience to reject Moloch's point of view.

Discussion

Essentially Belial is making an imaginative construction of a possible terrifying future, appealing to the audience's secret fears. This can be expressed in Classical terms in this way:

● he appeals to the audience's **ethos** by praising eternal thought (in spite of the fact that these thoughts are wandering aimlessly);

● he touches their **pathos**, or feelings of fear, though the shock of finding hope is despair, or by his imaginative construction of annihilation;

● he flatters their **logos** or rationality through all the questions and proofs (in spite of the fact that they contradict one another: God cannot be both the Victor and impotent).

The speech also uses several soundbites or figures, including antithesis (*hope/despair*); oxymoron (*sad cure*); alliteration and assonance (*wide womb of uncreated night*); rhetorical question (*who would lose?*); parallel construction (*how he can ... that he never will*), and a final antithesis (*saves/To punish*).

The Poem as an Epic

Recognizing the Characteristics of Epic and Myth

There are three principal Classical epics, Homer's *Iliad* and *Odyssey* (Greek, possibly 800 BC), and Vergil's *Aeneid* (Latin, First century BC; see Appendix pp.196–7). These are very long narrative poems giving accounts of the exploits of the chief heroes and gods of their national culture; they can be seen as statements expressive of that culture. Epics of different kinds had been written since the Classical past, for example Dante's *Divine Comedy* (Italy, 1321), Ariosto's *Orlando Furioso* (Italy, 1532), and Spenser's *Fairie Queene* (England, 1589). All of these influenced Milton, but he was inspired particularly by Ariosto's example to try not just to write a long narrative poem, but to copy the Classical form itself in a modern language, and even to make that language more Classical so that:

> I might perhaps leave something so written to aftertimes, as they should not willingly let it die ... I applied myself to that resolution which Ariosto followed ... to fix all the industry and art I could unite to the adorning of my native tongue.
>
> > (*The Reason of Church Government*).

Having eventually decided on the language and form he wanted to write in, Milton deliberated long about a subject, and decided that the Old Testament should provide the historical basis for his epic as this is the first part of human history as a whole. Books I and II are full of Old Testament characters and stories, particularly the story of Moses' Flight from Egypt, and the early history of the Jews when they were establishing themselves in a pagan land and constantly following their pagan gods. He added to his Biblical sources his immense accumulation of Classical and modern learning, so the poem is also full of allusions to the heroic leadership of Aeneas, and the intrepid explorations of Ulysses (see pp.171-2). But above all, he used his imagination to transform all these elements of epic, myth, and history into a personal vision of the battle between good and evil.

The principal narratives of his epic, however, involve the supernatural, and are not history so much as myth. The Classical epic poets had also included the supernatural in their epics, because their 'historical' heroes had been aided by gods whom we often see debating the issues in Heaven. In his unorthodox and unpublished religious book, *De Doctrina Christiana*, Milton drew a distinction between the kind of truth the Bible revealed about natural and supernatural characters. When we read about the natural characters we can believe what it says is history, but when we read about the supernatural, we cannot expect it to be more than accommodated truth, the kind of inspired poetic fables used by Moses, who supposedly wrote *Genesis*. Such fables or myths answer questions about our origins or our human predicament, but do so in a different way from history, because their underlying meaning is more important than their literal narrative. Milton uses two myths, the stories of the fall of Satan and the fall of Man, and both of these answer the same question: 'if God is good, why did evil come into the world?' Milton may or may not have believed in the literal existence of Satan; what he clearly did believe was the objective existence of evil, and the myths both demonstrate that this evil was not invented by God, but arises from false choices within the mind of free individuals. Milton therefore sees himself as the successor to Moses (as he says in his invocation, I 8), inspired by the same Holy Spirit to elaborate the myths of the Bible so as to teach an inner truth about *the ways of God* (I 26).

Activity

Read I 507–21 with the relevant notes. How does the story of the Titans compare with the story of the fall of Satan, and what question about our lives does it answer?

Discussion

Greek heroes and gods seem to have benefited from exercising the very qualities which landed Satan in Hell. The Titans successfully rebelled against their father Uranus, though they were in turn deposed by their children, *So Jove usurping reigned* (514). Perhaps such stories mirror the inevitable conflict between parents and children, and answer the question 'how can we grow up and achieve freedom?' In the Titans' case it was by disobedience and rebellion against their father; in Satan's case it would have been by remaining loyal to his father. In these terms, the story of Satan is essentially a negative account of Man's developing relationship with his parents, and the story of Adam, who also disobeys, a positive one.

Epic Similes

As was pointed out on p.157 and p.167 above, some of the characteristics of Milton's style, in particular his Latinate English and his rhetorical speeches, are a deliberate imitation of epic style: the formal grandeur which had made even such a long poem as the *Iliad* memorable for generations before it was written down. Milton made his poem even more like an epic by introducing epic similes. Both Homer and Vergil used extended similes (for example, Homer compares Achilles' shield to the whole world), but Milton's are more like Vergil's, because there is more than one point of correspondence between the image and its object. For example, many of the epic similes in Book I are about Satan's size: Leviathan and the moon are both enormous (like Satan), but they are all also shifty in some way (also like Satan): Leviathan tricks sailors into thinking him an island; the moon presides over the hours of darkness when such things happen, and can even block out the sun in daytime; and Satan deceives not only his fellow angels and Mankind, but himself, hiding the light of truth. These considerations mean that Satan seems both impressive and not impressive; his heroic stature is undermined.

As we read Books I and II, we notice certain repeated patterns in the similes, notably the use of night and the moon, and the use of sea-voyages. Two stories keep returning as well: the story of the Titans and the story of Moses. The Greek myth of the Titans is similar to the Christian myth of the fall of the angels, because it is about how the Titan gods deposed their father-king, but were then themselves deposed by their children (see note to I 196–200). Moses, whose story is told in *Exodus,* is a kind of opposite to Satan, for he leads the Jews out of slavery in Egypt to their own Promised Land, whereas Satan can only lead his fallen angels to steal Mankind's promised land. The angels can also be compared to the Egyptians in the story, who suffered ten plagues before they would release the Jews, and were then drowned in the Red Sea as they attempted to pursue them (see note to I 307). The use of similar material for the epic similes gives the poem cohesion.

Some of the epic similes			
	Book I		Book 2
Leviathan	197–209	Tempest at sea	285–90
Volcano	238	Clouds and sun	488–95
Moon	287–91	Hercules	542–6
Fallen leaves	301–3	Obscured sun	594–600
Red Sea	304–11	Spice fleet	636–42
Locusts	338–43	Black clouds	714–8
Burnt pines	612–15	Bellona	921–7
Bees/Pygmies/elves	768–87	Griffon	943–7

Activity

Look up two similes which involve the moon: I 284–91; I 768–87. What is the principal point of comparison between the simile and the thing described? What is the secondary or hidden comparison?

Discussion

I 284–91: the principal point of comparison is size – the shield is very big – but the moon is also given negative connotations (*spotty*) and is diminished in importance by being seen through a telescope (*optic glass*). The size-shifting continues up to 307: Satan's spear is bigger than the tallest pine tree, but the angels are compared first to leaves, and then to water-weed (*scattered sedge*), as if Milton were now seeing them through the wrong end of his telescope. Does this suggest Milton's scorn? Or does it give them the attractiveness of natural objects? Or does it simply suggest the dream-like world we have entered where nothing stays the same for long?

I 781–7: Here the angels have actually shrunk to the size of tiny elves, so again the principal point of comparison is size. However, the connotations are more sinister. They are like elves who dance below the moon, making wicked plans which frighten the *benighted peasant*, just as the fallen angels will soon be plotting to harm Mankind. Moreover, the elves are enjoying themselves, which suggests the angels' sense of relief and recovered self-esteem.

Narrative Features of Epic

Besides being written in an elevated style and including long similes, epic contained characteristic narrative features and set pieces. Here are some which Milton adapts:

● invocations to his Muse, or divine inspiration, as at I 6.

● starting the story in the middle, *in media res*. The war in Heaven has already happened, and the temptation of Man is to come, when the action begins at I 50.

● centring the story on heroes. Although he is evil, Satan has a good deal in common with the typical Classical hero, particularly Aeneas, the hero of the *Aeneid*. Rather like Satan, he leads his defeated forces away from burning Troy, leaves most of them resting in Sicily, and virtually alone finds the site of Rome and founds a new kingdom. Moreover, in Book I Satan seems to have the Classical virtues associated with heroes: Homer describes the compassion of Agamemnon who, like Satan, sheds tears over his army's pain, the courage of Hector when faced by overwhelming odds, and the endurance and resourcefulness of Ulysses. But one can notice important differences between Satan and such heroes. For example, Satan's aim is not to found his own kingdom so much as to deprive others of theirs, and his heroic individuality does not serve God (as Aeneas' did), but his own pride.

● including a procession of heroes followed (eventually) by a battle. Milton's procession begins at I 376, preceded by a new invocation to the Muse. The battle, which has already occurred, occupies Book VI.

● including accounts of councils. The debate in Book II of *Paradise Lost* is influenced by Book II 50–397 of the *Iliad*, where the Greeks are debating whether or not to continue the war against Troy. Here, too, the promoters of peace (Agamemnon and Thersites) nearly carry the day, and it is only with difficulty that Ulysses stops their flight by attacking their cowardice.

● including a description of the Underworld. The most famous book of the *Aeneid*, Book VI, shows Aeneas visiting the Underworld (see Appendix pp.196-7). There he finds the four rivers mentioned by Milton (II 575), and watches the games of the glorious dead (see *P.L.* II 528-46).

● including a voyage, such as that which occupies much of the *Odyssey* (see II 629, particularly noting the similes which constantly associate Satan with the sea).

Activity

Analyse the section from *Aeneid VI* which is printed in the Appendix pp.196–7. How many features does it have in common with the description of Hell in II 570–628, and are there any notable differences?

Discussion

This exercise is too long to complete here, but your points of comparison and difference could focus on the following features:

● the dream-like, almost surreal sights: for example Vergil's *shadowy giant elm* with its dream-leaves (11–13), or Milton's ice landscape with its heaps of hail (589–90).

● the inclusion in both of emotions: for example, in Vergil Grief and Care are like human beings sleeping before the gates of *Orcus* (Hell, 1–2), and Milton follows Classical tradition in linking each river in Hell with a particular emotion (576–9).

● the monsters: for example both mention the Chimera (whose body was composed of several beasts) and the snake-haired Gorgon (Vergil,17–19; Milton, 628). In Milton this links to the theme of false creativity discussed on p.163.

● the similes: Vergil compares the numerous dead, who long to enter their final place of rest, with fallen leaves and migrating birds (35–8). Milton's Hell is not a place of rest (indeed the whole passage suggests restlessness; see p.146), though he does use the image of fallen leaves at I 301–3. Do you think this image has a different effect in each poem?

The Characters

Dramatic Characterization of the Fallen Angels

Readers of Books I and II often raise the following questions: If God created a good Heaven, why did so many angels rebel? Why did he then punish them eternally in a specially-prepared torture chamber, instead of forgiving them? Why are all the angels sharing the same punishment, when some were clearly leaders and others followers? Questions such as these are provoked because Milton has made Satan and his army so real to us that we cannot help viewing them as human. But really they are representations of evil qualities like deceit, malice, and greed, just as God is a representation of truth and goodness (see headnote to I 376-521). This last section will explore Milton's characterization of the angels, to protect you from being too attracted to them.

Satan's Character

When we are first introduced to Satan it is with the words *guile, envy, revenge,* and *pride* (I 34-6). This prepares us to meet a villain, and yet when he appears he seems much more like a hero. In spite of his own shock and pain, he cheers and encourages his army, and although you might feel he is leading them in the wrong direction, Beëlzebub seems to be right when he says that Satan's voice is *their liveliest pledge/Of hope* (I 274-5). Moreover, he is clearly superior to them in character as well as position; while they wait passively for his return, he is actively meeting danger and carrying out his plans. Indeed, when Milton sums up his character (I 599-605) he uses the words *dauntless courage, remorse,* and *passion,* as well as the words *revenge, pride,* and *cruel.* He seems therefore to be both evil and good at the same time. How can this be explained, and is he the villain or the hero of the poem?

Activity

Can you find any evidence in the parts of the poem you have read for the qualities listed at I 34–36: *guile, envy,* and *revenge*; and for those listed at I 599–605: *dauntless courage, remorse,* and *passion*?

Discussion

There are several examples of Satan showing these qualities; the following are a selection:

guile   Perhaps the clearest example is the conversation between Satan and Sin. He reveals what is probably the truth when he says (II 745) he never saw *Sight more detestable* than Sin and Death. Yet when she has explained that she holds the key to his escape from Hell, he calls her his *dear daughter* (817) and tells her that his mission to Earth is simply to advance her and her son's interests.

revenge   Virtually every speech Satan makes can be seen as motivated by his desire to revenge himself on God for his humiliation and punishment. For example, at I 167 he discusses what behaviour *shall grieve him*, and at I 661 he seems to be speaking for all the fallen angels when he promises to continue the war *for who can think submission*? Only Moloch expresses a similar open hatred of God.

envy   Here the clearest example is Satan's jealousy of Mankind, expressed at, for example, I 654, where he resents the *favour* God shows these upstarts.

dauntless courage (fearless courage)   Satan has so little sense of fear that not even Death can frighten him (*Satan stood/Unterrified*, II 707–8). His determination to cross Chaos in spite of its terrifying confusion is even more impressive (II 918–27).

remorse and passion   At the place from which this quotation was taken (I 605), Satan even seems to regret having caused his followers to *have their lot in pain* (I 608). This seems to show not only a genuine affection for them, but a realization of his responsibility in wrong-doing. He even weeps for them. Do you agree with F.T. Prince, who said in his edition (see p.vi) that *this is one of the most moving touches in Milton's presentation of him as a tragic character*, or do you feel this is simply another example of *guile*?

The combination of good and evil in Satan attracts our interest and our compassion; they make him feel like a human being. In the section on Milton's religious ideas (see pp.146–7), it was suggested that Satan has misdirected his good, angelic qualities to the wrong end by replacing the love of God by the love of himself, and that this pride is the essence of his evil. His pride is indeed all-consuming; having failed to overthrow God, he will do anything to get revenge, including destroying innocent Mankind simply because God loves them. And yet this pride is itself partly heroic; heroes are essentially people who believe in themselves in spite of overwhelming odds. Is it not also his *considerate pride* (I 603) (well-considered pride) which makes him consider and help his fellow-angels, even if he does so in order that they should help him achieve his ambition? Should we admire his ambition for making him determined, resourceful, and brave? Or should we condemn it for making him a tyrant who is simply using his army to achieve his own ambitions and revenge? The bad is part of this good, for under the heroic qualities of courage, compassion, and eloquence are egotism, pride, cunning, and deceitfulness.

In fact, his deceitfulness is as significant as his pride. Practically the first thing we are told about him is that he is *Vaunting aloud, but racked with deep despair* (I 126). His words here do not reveal his thoughts; even to his *nearest mate* (I 192) he must put on some sort of front. Such *vaunting* not only distracts him from despair; it is also part of his constant manipulation of others. He encourages, sneers, argues, advises, and bullies his fellow angels into obedience, while all the time promoting himself as their saviour (can you find examples of these techniques?). But does Milton mean us to think that he is also deceiving himself, and that he really believes he can revenge himself upon God?

Activity

Look closely at the speech with which Satan opens the debate in Hell (II 11–42). Make a list of all the lies he tells, and say which ones we might suppose he himself believes.

Discussion

Satan's lies are not all of the same kind. Some seem to be only half-conscious, some are expedient half-truths designed to encourage his army, and some are deliberate falsehoods designed to manipulate them. The speech opens with flattery, though it is no longer true that the angels are *Powers and Dominions, deities of heaven* (11). It is only half true to say they are *oppressed and fallen* (13), as they had attempted to oppress God first. We may imagine that Satan himself believes that Heaven is not wholly *lost* (14), although in the soliloquy quoted and discussed below he says the opposite. It is very misleading for him to claim that *just right and fixed laws* (18) made him their leader, as this position was given him by God, and it is only partly true that his position is unrivalled, as he never gives them the opportunity to choose (19) a rival. It is quite untrue that Heaven is their *just inheritance* (38) or that their defeat will make them *surer to prosper* (39). Most serious of all, he is only pretending to ask their advice, and is already limiting the question under debate to *how* and not *whether* they continue the war. In fact they do debate whether to continue the war, and even opt for peace, and it requires all Beëlzebub's powers of persuasion and deceit to make them vote for what Satan has already decided to do.

Satan's Soliloquy

Most of the time we can only guess at what Satan is really supposed to be thinking, because he is so complex and deceitful, so *subtle* (II 815). However, in Book IV, when he makes his next appearance, he is alone for the first time. He speaks his first soliloquy sitting on the Sun, surveying the Earth with envy and regret. This speech is so important and useful that I am going to quote parts of it here, using Milton's line numbers from Book IV so that you can refer back to the complete speech. It is a revelation of the 'real' Satan underneath the bluster and the lies. He begins by admitting the astonishing fact that he still loves God, and that his happiness ended when:

> pride and worse ambition threw me down
> Warring in heaven against heaven's matchless king:
> Ah wherefore! He deserved no such return
> From me, whom he created what I was
> In that bright eminence, and with his good
> Upbraided none; nor was his service hard.
> What could be less than to afford him praise,
> The easiest recompense, and pay him thanks,
> How due! (40–48)

This underlying love of God explains why he is so set on revenge because it explains why he cares so much that God had humiliated and rejected him. Now that he is calling things by their true names, we see that he regrets his crime, misses the *happy fields* (I 249) of Heaven, and above all feels *wrath* at his humiliation and *despair* that he has lost God's love (IV 74). He continues to *upbraid* (scold, IV 45) himself:

> Nay cursed be thou; since against his thy will
> Chose freely what it now so justly rues.
> Me miserable! Which way shall I fly
> Infinite wrath, and infinite despair?
> Which way I fly is hell; myself am hell;
> And in the lowest deep a lower deep
> Still threatening to devour me opens wide,
> To which the hell I suffer seems a heaven.   (71–78)

Like Mephistopheles in *Dr. Faustus* (see Appendix pp.197-8), he recognizes that the true Hell is within his own mind; he made, and will always make *a Hell of Heaven* in spite of his boast (I 255) that he can make *a Heaven of Hell*. His nature is progressing not towards creative good, but towards self-destructive evil.

At this point he confronts the unspoken question behind Books I and II: should he ask God to restore him and the other angels to Heaven? He now gives his reasons for answering 'no'. The first reason is that he is too proud:

> O then at last relent: is there no place
> Left for repentance, none for pardon left?
> None left but by submission; and that word
> Disdain forbids me, and my dread of shame
> Among the spirits beneath, whom I seduced ...   (79–83)

His second, more deadly reason is that he feels he has no choice. He feels, in fact, that he is 'programmed' to revolt, and so is denying free will to himself, as he denied it to his followers. It is a characteristic of all the fallen angels to deny freedom, and to say that fate, and not God, controls the Universe (for example, both Belial and Mammon say their fate keeps them in Hell, II 197 and 232). Nothing more clearly demonstrates slavery to sin than this inability to believe in free choice and imagine a better future:

> But say I could repent, and could obtain
> By act of grace my former state; how soon

> Would highth recall high thoughts, how soon unsay
> What feigned submission swore; ...
>
> So farewell hope, and with hope farewell fear,
> Farewell remorse: all good to me is lost;
> Evil be thou my good; by thee at least
> Divided empire with Heaven's king I hold
> By thee, and more than half perhaps will reign;
> As men ere long, and this new world shall know.　　　(108–113)

The soliloquy ends in despair, a despair which expresses the best side of Satan: his recognition of God's goodness, and so his underlying love of him. This contrasts sharply with the hatred he has been expressing for God in Books I and II, when God was his *Foe*, the *Tempter*, the *Victor*, and worse. If he really believed that God was evil he would not suffer to have lost his love, nor care so much about hurting him in return. It is because he is essentially good that he suffers, and because of his suffering that we pity him in spite of his malice.

Beëlzebub, Moloch, Mammon, Belial, and the Other Leaders

Milton finds the names for his chief fallen angels from the Bible though only Satan and Beëlzebub were traditional names for devils. Satan has many appearances in the Bible (see p.195); for example, it is he who pauses in *walking up and down in the Earth* to tempt patient Job (*Job* 1:7). His name probably means *enemy*, a name which he prefers to give to God. Beëlzebub is the *Lord of the Flies* or the *Prince of Demons* (*Matthew* 12:24). Belial and Mammon are not specific devils, but words used in the Bible to epitomize particular vices: Belial suggests depravity and licence (*1 Samuel* 2:12-17); Mammon, greed and worldly values (*Matthew* 6:24). To provide names for the other captains, Milton is using an old tradition that the fallen angels, *long after* (I 383) the events described in Book I, became the pagan gods (see headnote to I 376-521). Moloch was the Sun-god of the Ammonites (*2 Kings* 23), and the other leaders in the parade of the gods are mostly taken from the same part of the Bible, where the Jews are surrounded by, and often tempted to worship, pagan gods. Milton, in fact, focuses on moments when God's chosen people, the Jews, took these pagan gods into their own holy places, and purposely degraded themselves by indulging in the vices such gods encouraged: violence, lust, self-indulgence, and so forth.

The chiefs, however, do retain some angelic qualities. Beëlzebub is intelligent; he alone realizes that God may have his own reasons for keeping them alive (I 145-52), and he shows *deliberation ... and public care ... majestic* when he turns round the whole feeling of the debate by sneering at the fallen angels' desire to settle quietly in Hell, and introduces Satan's plan to seduce Mankind in words which make it irresistible. Moloch retains the integrity and simple-mindedness of the true general. He is the only fallen angel besides Satan to really feel despair because he genuinely recognizes God's superiority (II 45-50), though his speech suggests the cruelty of a god who eats human babies (I 392-9). Belial is attractive to look at, *graceful and humane* (II 109); if we were to put him in a modern setting, he would be charming a girl on his mobile phone, while kicking a beggar into the gutter without even removing the cigarette from his lips. He is also attractive in a more subtle way, because he is the most eloquent speaker, and his evocation of our human fears of annihilation or torture ring true. Mammon *the least erected spirit that fell* (I 679) is also surprisingly eloquent, but his promise that *Our torments also may in length of time/Become our elements* (II 274-5, see also II 215-220 where Belial makes the same point) shows that he is embracing his own degradation. It is only the fallen angels who continue to suffer pain and despair, like Satan, Moloch, and perhaps Beëlzebub, who continue to resemble the angels they once were. If you read on through the whole poem, you will see Satan gradually lose this capacity to see the truth and to suffer, and become shallow and merely spiteful.

Activity

Look closely at II 555–628, in which the fallen angels are occupying themselves while Satan is away, and find words which suggest *wandering* and *restlessness*. What reasons can you find for this state of mind?

Discussion

Heaven is changeless, but in Hell everything is in turmoil, and everyone is busy but without real direction. Milton believed that the proper end to all activities should be God or goodness (see pp.146–7), so the fallen angels are missing not only Satan, but God. Their philosophy does not lead to a conclusion *in wandering mazes lost* (561), which recalls Belial's description of thoughts which *wander through eternity* (II 148) without reaching back to God. The landscape they wander about in reflects the turmoil in their minds, as it is beaten by *perpetual storms/Of whirlwind and dire hail* (588–9), and they find there no rest (618; compare I 65–6 where we are told that *peace/And rest can never dwell* in Hell). We should contrast Jesus' offer to the heavy-laden *I will give you rest* (*Matthew* 11:28). Is Satan in any way as restless and without direction as his fellow angels? Does he wander through Chaos, or take control of his way?

Allegorical Characters (Sin and Death, Chaos and Night)

If the devils are something between characters and representatives of vice, Sin and Death are much less human, much more personifications, and the story of their birth is an **allegory** (a symbolic story or picture in which every detail has a meaning which must be interpreted). To see them as characters would make Sin, in particular, too sympathetic. Her predicament is by any human standards both pitiable and unjustly inflicted. One can quite understand why she disobeys a God *who hates me* (II 857). But we should read her and Death as a detailed allegory of these words from *The Epistle of James*:

> Then when lust hath conceived, it bringeth forth sin, and sin, when
> it is finished, bringeth forth death.   (*James* 1:15)

Satan's *bold conspiracy against Heaven's King* (II 251) can be seen as a kind of *lust* or desire for power. It leaps out of his head in the form of a woman, as a kind of 'false creation' (see p.163) opposite to Divine creation; in effect Satan, not God, invented sin. Satan then falls in love with his own creation (*Thyself in me thy perfect image viewing*, II 164), which demonstrates allegorically that sin is a kind of self-love. Their child is Death, because all sin destroys man's healthy nature. The theme of self-reflection is continued when Death himself rapes his mother, and their children, the hell-hounds, continue the rape by kennelling in her *womb* (798). Self-love can only lead to inner chaos and decay, and to the false creativity which is the opposite of true creative love (see p.163).

On a mythic level, however, this sin is more significant than ordinary human acts of sin. The sin of Adam and Eve *brought death into the world* and, as Satan is responsible for their committing that sin, he is shown here as the father of Death, and about to release Death and Sin into the world. This is allegorized when they build a road for them to get to Earth to devour Mankind, and for sinners to travel down to Hell for punishment (II 1023-33). Satan, Sin, and Death form a kind of unity, a demon Trinity, an opposite to the Holy Trinity of Father, Son, and Holy Spirit, and Sin even looks forward to sitting on Satan's right, as Christ sits on God's right hand at II 879 (see *Luke* 22:69).

Chaos and Night are less complex. Milton is using the Classical idea that matter, in a very confused and violent form, existed before the creation of the Universe (see p.148). To give such a disordered world a ruler would be a contradiction in terms, so Milton invents an *anarch* (II 988, from *anarchy*, meaning 'without rule'), who does not so much rule as *embroils the fray* (II 908). His age suggests not only that Chaos precedes all the worlds with form (such as Hell and Earth), but also that he is weak and incompetent (his speech is *faltering*, II 989), and unable to prevent God from raiding his territory to create new worlds. Logically, Chaos should be a good, or at least a neutral character, since matter all comes ultimately from God. But it suits Milton's plot to make him a supporter of Satan, once the *subtle fiend* has promised to reduce Earth to *her original darkness and your sway* (II 984). Chaos does not realize that Satan will say anything to get his help in finding Earth, and that if this promise comes true at all, it will only be figuratively. Milton follows his sources (particularly Hesiod, a Greek writer on the gods) in giving Chaos a *consort* or wife, Night. She is equally negative, suggesting the darkness which is the opposite to God and to ordered life. Like Sin, she is female, suspect, and easily deceived (see discussion on the female body, pp.162-3). They are surrounded by other personifications who are clearly influenced by earlier descriptions of Chaos, and by Vergil's account of the Underworld (II 963-7: see Appendix pp.196-7). But the real ruler in this half-imaginary world is Chance (II 910), because any other rule would imply some kind of order. It is only by chance that Satan crosses the Underworld at all (II 935). The story should be read literally - this is a real journey across a real space - but these personified characters do not have the realism of Satan or even Sin, and we cannot care about them in the same way.

Activity

What does the *fatal key* (II 871) suggest to you?

Discussion

Keys are often symbolic, partly because the insertion of a key in a door suggests the sexual act. This key was given to Sin by God (II 775), with *charge* to keep the devils shut inside Hell. Once Satan realizes this (II 815), he uses his most persuasive flattery and promises (which are not altogether deceitful) to get her to disobey God and open the door. This directly anticipates his later realization that the fruit of the forbidden tree is the 'key' to the fall of Mankind, and that he must use all his power to persuade Eve (like Sin, a woman) to eat it. Allegorically then, the key, like the fruit, represents the choice between good and evil — the choice which is itself the key to understanding the poem as a whole.

So we have come to the end of these Approaches to the text, and I hope you will now feel able not only to enjoy Books I and II, but also to go on and read the rest of the poem, not because it is a classic, but because it is so exciting and so real.

A Synopsis of *Paradise Lost*

One can get some idea of the story of the whole poem by reading through the arguments which introduce each book. The overall plan is as follows:

Book I   Satan and his followers are shown where they have been hurled by God, lying on the burning lake in the middle of Hell. Satan flies off the lake, then returns to the lakeside and calls his army together. The chief devils are named; they build Pandæmonium.

Book II   The chief angels debate what to do next; they adopt Satan's plan of revenging themselves on Man rather than on God. Satan flies off to Earth, meeting Sin and Death at the gates of Hell; they follow him and build a road to Earth.

Book III   Milton laments his loss of sight. God and his Son watch what the devils are doing and explain how they will bring good out of evil, the Son offering himself as a sacrifice.

Book IV   Satan laments his loss of Heaven and reveals his motives for betraying Man. The Garden of Eden is described, and Satan sees Adam and Eve there, who praise God and make love innocently. Satan tries to tempt Eve while she is asleep, but is caught by Gabriel and expelled from the garden.

Book V   Raphael visits Adam and Eve and tells them the story of Satan's rebellion, including the plotting by night, and the resistance of one angel, Abdiel.

Book VI   Raphael then describes the war in Heaven and warns Adam and Eve about Satan's presence and his plans to seduce them from obedience.

Book VII   Raphael describes the creation of the world and promises that Adam and Eve will one day ascend to Heaven themselves, *if ye be found /Obedient.*

Book VIII   Adam and Raphael discuss cosmology, and Adam relates to Raphael how he was created, confessing privately to him that he loves Eve too much.

Book IX   After another invocation to the Muse, Milton describes how Eve persuades Adam to let her work in the Garden alone, how she meets and is flattered by the serpent, and persuaded to eat the fruit of the forbidden tree. When she offers some to Adam, he decides to eat in order to die with her. Both of them are intoxicated by the fruit and make love lasciviously. They awake, and Adam and Eve quarrel and blame each other for their predicament.

Book X   The Son is sent to judge and clothe them, and promises them a future. Satan returns to Pandæmonium, but his boasting of success prompts a *universal hiss* as they are all suddenly turned into snakes (a periodic punishment for them). Sin and Death take possession of the Earth and angels tilt the world to alter the seasons. Eve persuades Adam to ask God for pardon.

Book XI   God accepts Adam and Eve's repentance, and Michael is sent to show Adam and Eve the hideous effects of the Fall in human suffering and disease. He tells them the story of Man's repeated sins until the Flood.

Book XII   Michael continues the story until the Redemption by Christ, and then sends Adam and Eve out into the fallen world:

> Some natural tears they dropped, but wiped them soon;
> The world was all before them, where to choose
> Their place of rest, and Providence their guide;
> They hand in hand with wandering steps and slow,
> Through Eden took their solitary way.   (XII 645–9)

Chronology of Milton's Life

1603–25	Reign of James I
1608	John Milton born (9 December) in London
1620–25	Attends St. Paul's School, London
1625–49	Reign of Charles I
1625–32	Studies at Christ's College, Cambridge (MA 1632)
1632–8	Reading and writing poetry mostly at Horton, Bucks., with his parents; *Comus* performed 1634; mother dies 1637
1638–9	Milton travels to France and Italy
1639	Milton returns to London, and starts tutoring boys (including his nephews, Edward and John Phillips)
1641	Milton begins writing pamphlets on Church Government
1642	Marries Mary Powell; she returns to her parents' house within two months, partly because Civil War begins
1643–5	Publishes *Divorce Tracts*; Mary returns to him 1645; he also publishes *Areopagitica* (1644) and his *Poems* (1645)
1646	Royalists finally surrender
1647	Father dies
1649	Charles I executed; Milton publishes political pamphlets, including *Tenure of King and Magistrates* (1649) and two *Defences of the English People* (1651 and 1654); appointed Secretary for the Foreign Tongues to the Commonwealth
1652	Milton becomes blind; wife dies when third daughter born
1653	Milton allowed a substitute for the Secretaryship and partially retires from public life
1656–8	Marries Catherine Woodstock who dies within two years; begins writing *Paradise Lost* about 1658
1660	Restoration of Charles II; Milton briefly imprisoned for publishing *Ready and Easy Way to Establish a Free Commonwealth* (1659)
1663	Marries Elizabeth Minshull
1665–6	Great Plague (1665) and Great Fire of London (1666)
1667	Publication of *Paradise Lost* Edition 1
1671	Publication of *Samson Agonistes* and *Paradise Regained*
1674	Publication of *Paradise Lost* Edition II. Milton dies of gout

Further Reading

Editions and Tapes

There are scholarly editions of *Paradise Lost I and II* by F.T. Prince (Oxford University Press, 1962), and by John Broadbent (Cambridge University Press, 1972), both with detailed notes and introductions. There are numerous editions of the whole poem and other works, including *The Works of John Milton*, edited by John Carey and Alastair Fowler (Longman, 1968), and a Penguin selection, but you might prefer to hear the poem read to you on tape, such as *John Milton Paradise Lost* read by Anton Lesser (Naxos, 1994).

Historical and Biographical Studies

C.C. Brown, *John Milton: A Literary Life* (Macmillan, 1995).

Owen Chadwick, *The Reformation* (Penguin, 1964) (explains the religious context).

C. Hill, *The World Turned Upside-down* (Penguin, 1975) (discusses radical ideas of the time, including Milton's).

G. Davies (ed.), *The Oxford History of England: 1603–1660* (Oxford University Press, 1955).

G. Clark (ed.), *The Oxford History of England: 1660–1714* (Oxford University Press, 1959).

P. Levi, *Eden Revisited: The Public and Private Life of John Milton* (Macmillan, 1996).

L. Potter, *A Preface to Milton* (Longman, 1986) (a lively account of Milton's life and poetry).

A.N. Wilson, *A Life of John Milton* (Mandarin, 1996).

D. Wooton (ed.), *Divine Right and Democracy: An Anthology of Political Writing in Stuart England* (Penguin, 1986).

Short Introductions to the Poem

F.C. Blessington, *Paradise Lost: A Student Companion* (Twyne, 1988) (a school handbook).

J. Broadbent, *Paradise Lost: An Introduction* (Cambridge University Press, 1972) (a detailed introduction).

D. Daiches, *Milton's Paradise Lost* (Arnold, 1983) (a book-by-book commentary).

E. Lowenstein, *Milton's Paradise Lost* (Landmarks of World Literature, Cambridge University Press, 1993) (a detailed study of the background followed by a book-by-book commentary).

P. Weston, *John Milton: Paradise Lost* (Penguin Critical Studies, 1987) (an introductory section followed by book-by-book commentary).

Critical Essays

C. Belsey, *John Milton: Language, Gender, Power* (Blackwell, 1988) (this approaches the poem through modern critical theory).

D. Danielson (ed.), *The Cambridge Companion to Milton* (Cambridge University Press, 1989) (a series of new essays by different authors).

A.E. Dyson and J. Lovelock (eds.), *Milton's Paradise Lost: A Casebook* (Macmillan, 1973) (selections from famous interpretations).

W. Empson, *Milton's God* (Chatto, 1965) (this gives Satan's point of view).

R.T. Fallon, *Divided Empire* (Pennsylvania State University, 1995) (on politics in the poetry including an essay on 'To reign in Hell').

S. Fish, *Surprised by Sin* (University of California Press, 1971) (discusses some of Milton's self-contradictions).

B.K. Lewalski, *Paradise Lost and the Rhetoric of Literary Form* (University of California Press, 1992) (discusses use of rhetoric in the poem).

C.S. Lewis, *A Preface to Paradise Lost* (Oxford University Press, 1942) (a very readable discussion of the religious issues raised by the poem).

C. Martindale, *John Milton and the Transformation of Ancient Epic* (Croom Helm, 1986) (useful comparisons with Classical authors).

A. Patterson, *John Milton* (Longman's Critical Readings, 1992) (a sampling of recent critical appraoches to Milton).

C. Ricks, *Milton's Grand Style* (Oxford University Press, 1973) (a study of language).

J.M. Steadman, *Milton's Biblical and Classical Imagery* (Duquesne U.P., 1984).

J. Wittreich, *Feminist Milton* (Cornell University Press, 1987).

Tasks

It is important that from the start you make sure you understand precisely what Milton is saying. It is often helpful to rewrite the text into clear modern prose as you go (sharing the task with others if you can) until you are so used to Milton's style that it no longer seems necessary. I have not given this as a separate task.

1 What are the characteristic features of Milton's style in Books I and II?

2 Compare I 44-75 *or* II 587-628 with a description of Hell (or its equivalent) by another author taken from the Appendix. What have they in common? What are the advantages and limitations of Milton's method? (See Approaches p.172 for a model.)

3 How does the imagery used in I 587-608 contribute to our understanding of Satan's character of *archangel ruined*?

4 Look closely at the language used in I 670-99. What clues does Milton give to his view of the angels' activities in this scene?

5 How do the speeches made by Moloch, Belial, and Mammon in Book II relate to the descriptions which Milton gave of their characters in Book I?

6 Use some of Belial's and Mammon's arguments to explain why the angels seem to opt for *peace* at II 292, and then use some of Beëlzebub's counter-arguments to explain why they change to his plan by II 391.

7 Looking closely at the language and sound effects of II 920-50, explain how Milton dramatically conveys the difficulties of Satan's journey (see Approaches p.155).

8 Examine the ways in which Milton suggests that Satan and the other fallen angels, though magnificent, are both evil and doomed.

9 'Satan is a study of corrupted energy.' Discuss.

10 Milton often describes Satan as the 'subtle fiend'. Look at his

manipulation both of the truth and of other people in one or two speeches in Book II.

11 In Books I and II, do you feel that Milton was, as Blake claims, 'of the Devil's party without knowing it'? (The whole sentence is quoted on p.141.)

12 *Vaunting aloud, but racked with deep despair.* How does Milton convey these two sides to Satan's character? (You may find it helpful to refer to the parts of the Book IV soliloquy quoted in Approaches pp.176-8.)

13 Addison regarded Milton's Biblical and classical references as 'an unnecessary ostentation of learning.' How far do you agree?

14 How does a reading of Books I and II help you to define the nature of evil?

15 Discuss Milton's use of the female in Books I and II (look at Sin and Night and at the references to Hell as a female body; see Approaches pp.162-3).

16 Write an account of your own personal Hell, trying to incorporate some of those in the text and Appendix.

Class activities

Frieze from Book I Make a frieze of the chief fallen angels, now devils, using the Parade of I 376-521. You can draw them yourselves, or use magazine pictures to make collages (Astoreth, for example, is both male and female). Each student should be responsible for one god, and write a brief description in modern terms of his or her particular viciousness.

Debate from Book 2 Imagining that you yourselves are fallen angels, hold your own debate on the motion 'Should we continue the war against God?' As far as possible use the arguments expressed in II 43-283. The following points of view could be used as starting-points by different students, who should also incorporate additional quotations and modern examples:

1 The place. Should we *Accept this dark opprobrious den of shame* (58)?

2 Our death. Are we hoping for extinction *happier far/Than miserable to have eternal being?* (97) or would it be terrible to be *swallowed up and lost / In the wide womb of uncreated night* (150)?

3 Our suffering. Are we in fact suffering, or in despair *When ... the torturing hour/Calls us to penance* (91) or are we not too unhappy *Thus sitting, thus consulting, thus in arms* (164)?

4 Our freedom. Are we in *strictest bondage ... Under the inevitable curb* (321) or are we in effect freer than in the *splendid vassalage* of Heaven (250)?

5 Our creativity. Should we be trying to frustrate God's plans to *interrupt his joy* (371) or should we try to build something positive in Hell – *Nor want we skill ... and art* (272) ?

6 Our honour. Should we heroically continue the fight *Turning out tortures into horrid arms/Against the Torturer* (Moloch, 63), or is this pointless *since fate inevitable/subdues us* (198)?

A thirteenth century Medieval Hell from the Baptistry Church, Florence

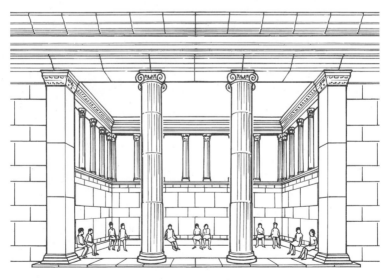

A sketch of a Greek building showing pilasters, Doric pillars, architrave, cornice and frieze

Hell Mouth from the Winchester Psalter, twelfth century. Note the key

Hell from *The Garden of Earthly Delights* by
Hieronymous Bosch (d.1516)

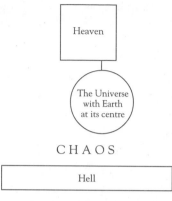

CHAOS

| Heaven |
| The Universe with Earth at its centre |
| Hell |

A sketch of Milton's Universe

An engraving by J. Barry of Satan summoning his legions, 1775

Appendix: Other Representations of Satan and Hell

Bible Passages Believed to Refer to Satan

From the *Authorized Version* of 1611; words from this translation often appear in Milton's poem, and it would have been well-known to his audience. I have also used this version in the Notes.

These parts of the Bible were stitched together to make the story of the fall of Satan and the fall of Man. Do you think Milton's characterization is consistent with these sources?

> *Revelation* 12:7–9: And there was war in Heaven; Michael and his angels fought against the dragon, and the dragon fought and his angels … And the dragon was cast out, that old serpent, called the Devil and Satan, who deceiveth the whole world; he was cast out into the Earth, and his angels were cast out with him.

> *Isaiah* 14:12–15: How art thou fallen from Heaven, O Lucifer, son of the morning! … For thou hast said in thine heart, I will ascend into Heaven, I will exalt my throne above the stars of God … I will ascend above the heights of the clouds, I will be like the most High. Yet thou shalt be brought down to Hell, to the sides of the pit.

> *Genesis* 3:1–6: Now the serpent was more subtle than any beast of the field which the Lord God had made. And he said unto the woman, Yea, hath God not said, you shall eat of every tree of the garden? And the woman said unto the serpent, We may eat of the fruit of the trees of the garden; But of the fruit of the tree that is in the midst of the garden, God hath said, Ye shall not eat of it, neither shall ye touch it, lest ye die. And the serpent said unto the woman, You shall not surely die; For God doth know that in the day ye eat thereof, then your eyes shall be opened, and ye shall be as Gods, knowing good and evil. And when the woman saw that the tree was good for food, and that it was pleasant to the eyes, and a tree to be desired to make one wise, she took of the fruit thereof, and did eat, and gave also unto her husband with her, and he did eat.

> *Genesis* 4:23: Therefore the Lord God sent him forth from the garden of Eden, to till the ground [from which he was made].

Vergil, *Aeneid* VI 271–314: Descent into the Underworld

From Vergil *Aeneid*, translated by Robert Fitzgerald (Random House, 1980).

Vergil's epic poem, the *Aeneid*, written in Rome in the First century BC, was an important influence on *Paradise Lost* (see Approaches p.167). The following passage, taken from Aeneas' descent into the Underworld, has several ideas which Milton used in Books I and II. Can you find them? This passage is compared with the the nightmare journey the angels make across Hell II 570–628 on p.172.

>   Before the entrance, in the jaws of Orcus,
>   Grief and avenging Cares have made their beds,
>   And pale Diseases and sad Age are there,
>   And Dread, and Hunger that sways men to crime,
> 5   And sordid Want – in shapes to affright the eyes –
>   And Death and Toil and Death's own brother, Sleep,
>   And the mind's evil joys; on the door sill
>   Death-bringer War, and iron cubicles
>   Of the Eumenides, and raving Discord,
> 10   Viperish hair bound up in gory bands.
>   In the courtyard a shadowy giant elm
>   Spreads ancient boughs, her ancient arms where dreams,
>   False dreams, the old tale goes, beneath each leaf
>   Cling and are numberless. There, too,
> 15   About the doorway forms of monsters crowd –
>   Briareus, and the Lernaean hydra
>   Hissing horribly, and the Chimaera
>   Breathing dangerous flames, and Gorgons, Harpies,
>   Huge Geryon, triple-bodied ghost.
> 20   Here, swept by sudden fear, drawing his sword,
>   Aeneas stood on guard with naked edge
>   Against them as they came. If his companion,
>   Knowing the truth, had not admonished him
>   How faint these lives were – empty images
> 25   Hovering bodiless – he had attacked
>   And cut his way through phantoms, empty air.

The path goes on from that place to the waves
Of Tartarus's Acheron …
Here a whole crowd came streaming to the bands,
30 Mothers and men, the forms with all life spent
Of heroes great in valour, boys and girls
Unmarried, and young sons laid on the pyre
Before their parents' eyes – as many souls
As leaves that yield their hold on boughs and fall
35 Through forests in the early frost of autumn,
Or as migrating birds from the open sea
That darken heaven when the cold season comes
And drives them overseas to sunlit lands
There all stood begging to be first across
40 And reached out longing hands to the far shore.

Marlowe, *Dr. Faustus*: The Hell Within

The English representation of the devil which had most influence on
Milton was that of Mephistopheles from Christopher Marlowe's play
Dr. Faustus (1592). Like Satan, Mephistopheles inhabits a mental as
well as a physical Hell, and he is unhappy because he is deprived of
God. In the following extracts Faustus, a magician, has just called
Satan from Hell and is questioning him. Compare the passage with I
25–8, or IV 32–113 where Satan also says that Hell is within his mind
(see Approaches p.162).

Faust.	Tell me, what is that Lucifer thy lord?
Meph.	Arch-regent and commander of all spirits.
Faus.	Was not that Lucifer an angel once?
Meph.	Yes Faustus, and most dearly loved of God.
Faus.	How comes it then that he is Prince of Devils?
Meph.	O, by aspiring pride and insolence,
	For which God threw him from the face of heaven.
Faus.	And what are you that live with Lucifer?
Meph.	Unhappy spirits that fell with Lucifer,
	Conspired against one God with Lucifer,
	And are forever damn'd with Lucifer.
Faus.	Where are you damn'd?

Meph.	In hell.
Faus.	How comes it then that thou are out of hell?
Meph.	Why, this is hell, nor am I out of it.
	Think'st thou that I, who saw the face of God
	And tasted the eternal joys of heaven,
	Are not tormented with ten thousand hells
	In being depriv'd of everlasting bliss?
	O Faustus, leave these frivolous demands
	Which strike a terror to my fainting soul.

I.3 70–85

Meph.	Now, Faustus, ask what thou wilt.
Faus.	First will I question with thee about hell.
	Tell me, where is the place that men call hell?
Meph.	Under the heavens.
Faus.	Ay, so are all things else; but whereabouts?
Meph.	Within the bowels of these elements,
	Where we are tortur'd and remain for ever.
	Hell hath no limits, nor is circumscrib'd
	In one self place, but where we are is hell
	And where hell is, there must we ever be;
	And so, to be short, when all the world dissolves
	And every creature shall be purify'd
	All places shall be hell that is not heaven.
Faus.	I think hell's a fable.
Meph.	Ay, think so still, till experience change thy mind.

I.5 115–30

J.P. Sartre, *Huis Clos*: A Modern Hell

(translated by Stuart Gilbert)

Sartre would not have accepted that there were victims in Hell; because for him what happens is inescapably one's own fault. The three people who find themselves together in Hell in *Huis Clos* (written in 1946 in Paris, and translated into English as *No exit* or *In Camera*), make Hell for each other because they have corrupted their own personalities so absolutely. When the play opens they are surprised to find no devils to torture them, only to discover later that they are themselves the torturers. Look at Satan's first sight of Hell (I 50–75) compared with

Garcin's (discussed in Approaches p.162). How do they try to hold on to their sense of self, and how is it suggested that they will continue to be a source of evil?

Garcin: But I say, where are the instruments of torture?
Valet: The what?
Garcin: The racks and red-hot pincers and all the other paraphernalia.
Valet: Ah, you must have your little joke, sir.
Garcin: My little joke? Oh, I see. No, I wasn't joking [*A short silence. He strolls around the room*] No mirrors, I notice. No windows. Only to be expected. And nothing breakable. [*Bursts out angrily*]. But, I damn it all! They might have left me my toothbrush!
Valet: That's good! so you haven't yet got over your – what do you call it? – sense of human dignity? Excuse me smiling.
Garcin: [*thumping ragefully the arm of an armchair*] I'll ask you to be more polite. I quite realize the position I'm in, but I won't tolerate ... [*He looks round*] And why should one want to see oneself in a looking-glass? But that bronze contraption on the mantelpiece, that's another story. I suppose there will be times when I stare my eyes out at it. Stare my eyes out – see what I mean? ... All right, lets put our cards on the table. I assure you I'm quite conscious of my position. Shall I tell you what it feels like? A man's drowning, choking, sinking by inches, till only his eyes are just above water, And what does he see? A bronze atrocity by – what's the fellow's name? – Barbedienne. A collector's piece. Like in a nightmare. That's their idea isn't it? ... No, I suppose you're under orders not to answer questions, and I won't insist. But don't forget, my man, I've a shrewd notion of what's coming to me, so don't you boast you've caught me off my guard. I'm facing up to the situation, facing up. [*he starts pacing the room again*] So that's that; no toothbrush. And no bed either. One never sleeps, I take it?
Valet: That's so.
Garcin: Just as I expected. *Why* should one sleep?

A. Hitler, *Speech to the Industry Club in Dusseldorf:* Awakening the Fallen

From B. MacArthur, (ed.) *The Penguin Book of Twentieth-Century Speeches* (Viking, 1992).

Hitler gave the speech from which this extract is taken during his first election campaign of 1932, when he promised a recovery from present economic hardship, caused by losing World War I, to those who would support the Nazi party. This activity was suggested by Helen Williams.

Today we stand at the turning-point of German's destiny. If the present development (degeneration) continues, Germany will one day of necessity land in Bolshevist chaos, but if this development is broken, then our people must be taken into a school of iron discipline and gradually freed ...

Even if another batch of 20 emergency decrees is rained down on our people, these will not stay the great line which leads to destruction, but if one day the road be discovered which leads upwards, then first of all the German people must be bent straight again. That is a process which none can escape! It is no good to say the proletarians are alone responsible. No, believe me, our whole German people of all ranks has a full measure of responsibility for our collapse – some because they willed it and have consciously sought to bring it about, the others because they looked on and were too weak to stop our downfall. In history the failure to act is weighed as strictly as is the purpose or the deed. Today no-one can escape the obligation to complete the regeneration of the German body politic: everyone must show his personal sympathy, must take his place in the common effort.